Introduction to the
TRO BREIZ
a pilgrimage in Brittany

WENDY MEWES

Introduction to the
Tro Breiz
a pilgrimage in Brittany

published by Red Dog Books

ISBN: 978-0-9935815-9-5

© Wendy Mewes 2024

The right of Wendy Mewes to be identified as the author of this work is asserted in accordance with sections 77 and 78 of the Copyright Designs and Patents Act 1988

British Library Cataloguing-in-Publication Data
A catalogue record for this book is available
from the British Library

All rights reserved. The publisher's prior written consent is required
for any reproduction of this work, in part or in whole,
in any form whatsoever.

Illustrations © Wendy Mewes, unless otherwise indicated.

Red Dog Books is based in Somerset and in Brittany.
Enquiries should be addressed to the editorial office at
Red Dog Books, 29690 Berrien, France.

email: reddogbooks@orange.fr

www.reddogbooks.com

ABOUT THIS BOOK

The Tro Breiz is an unusual circular pilgrimage around Brittany. It connects the seven cathedrals of the seven founding saints, but the overall distance can vary enormously (from about 1000km) depending on the chosen routes. Waymarking on the ground is currently being developed by an association (see p.8) and various guidebooks (in French) are available, but it remains something of a do-it-yourself event for the shortest passage. This book is intended to give an indication of the potential for a personal journey. It provides the historical background of the Tro Breiz, the arrival of the Breton saints from Great Britain and their subsequent influence. It then offers an outline guide to each of the seven stages, with general maps showing the most direct versions of the route to provide a starting point for planning. A month is regarded as a typical commitment to complete the basic journey, but to include all the main religious sites along the way will add considerably to the total kilometres covered. The beauty and variety of the Breton landscape and the extraordinary depth of Breton culture and heritage will be in evidence on any part of this adventure. I walked the route in different seasons of the year (and all weathers) as the photographs indicate. My aim is to provide enough information here for readers to decide whether or not to take the plunge, and I hope the book will help to raise the general profile and international appeal of this historic pilgrimage.

Wendy Mewes

Acknowledgements

With thanks to all those who work so hard to maintain and vivify the routes of the Tro Breiz all around Brittany, and to the many local groups responsible for keeping chapels and churches accessible to visitors. I'm particularly grateful to Arnaud Lampire and Laurine Mourot at the Association Mon Tro Breizh for their kindness and support. Also my warm appreciation to friends who have joined me occasionally along the way, especially David Wright, Alan Montgomery, Lucy Kempton, Julia Kirby and Phil Watson.

WM

CONTENTS

ABOUT THIS BOOK . . . .
MAP 6
Introduction 7
Pilgrimage 10
Some relevant religious background 14
The Breton saints 19
Sacred Seven: the founding saints 25
Evidence 29
Modern revival 33

Saint-Pol-de-Léon (Saint Pol) 37

Stage 1 Saint Pol de Léon to Tréguier
Overview 40
Saint-Pol-de-Léon to Morlaix 41
Morlaix to Saint-Efflam 46
Saint-Efflam to Tréguier 50

Tréguier (Saint Tugdual & Saint Yves) 55

Stage 2 Tréguier to Saint Brieuc
Overview 58
Tréguier to the Abbaye de Beauport 59
Abbaye de Beauport to Saint-Brieuc 62

Saint-Brieuc (Saint Brieuc) 66

Stage 3 Saint-Brieuc to Saint-Malo
Overview 69
Saint-Brieuc to Lamballe 70
Lamballe to Dinan 74
Dinan to Saint-Malo 79

Saint-Malo (Saint Malo) 83

   Stage 4 Saint-Malo to Dol-de-Bretagne
   Overview 87
   Saint-Malo to Cancale 88
   Cancale to Dol-de-Bretagne 91

Dol-de-Bretagne (Saint Samson) 95

   Stage 5 Dol-de-Bretagne to Vannes
   Overview 99
   Dol-de-Bretagne to St-Méen-le-Grand 101
   St-Méen-le-Grand to Josselin 106
   Josselin to Vannes 111

Vannes (Saint Patern) 115

   Stage 6 Vannes to Quimper
   Overview 118
   Vannes to Erdeven 120
   Erdeven to Quimperlé 124
   Quimperlé to Quimper 130

Quimper (Saint Corentin) 134

   Stage 7 Quimper to Saint-Pol-de-Léon
   Overview 139
   Quimper to Menez Hom 140
   Menez Hom to Commana 144
   The Parish Closes 147
   Commana to Saint-Pol-de-Léon 150

PRACTICAL INFORMATION 153

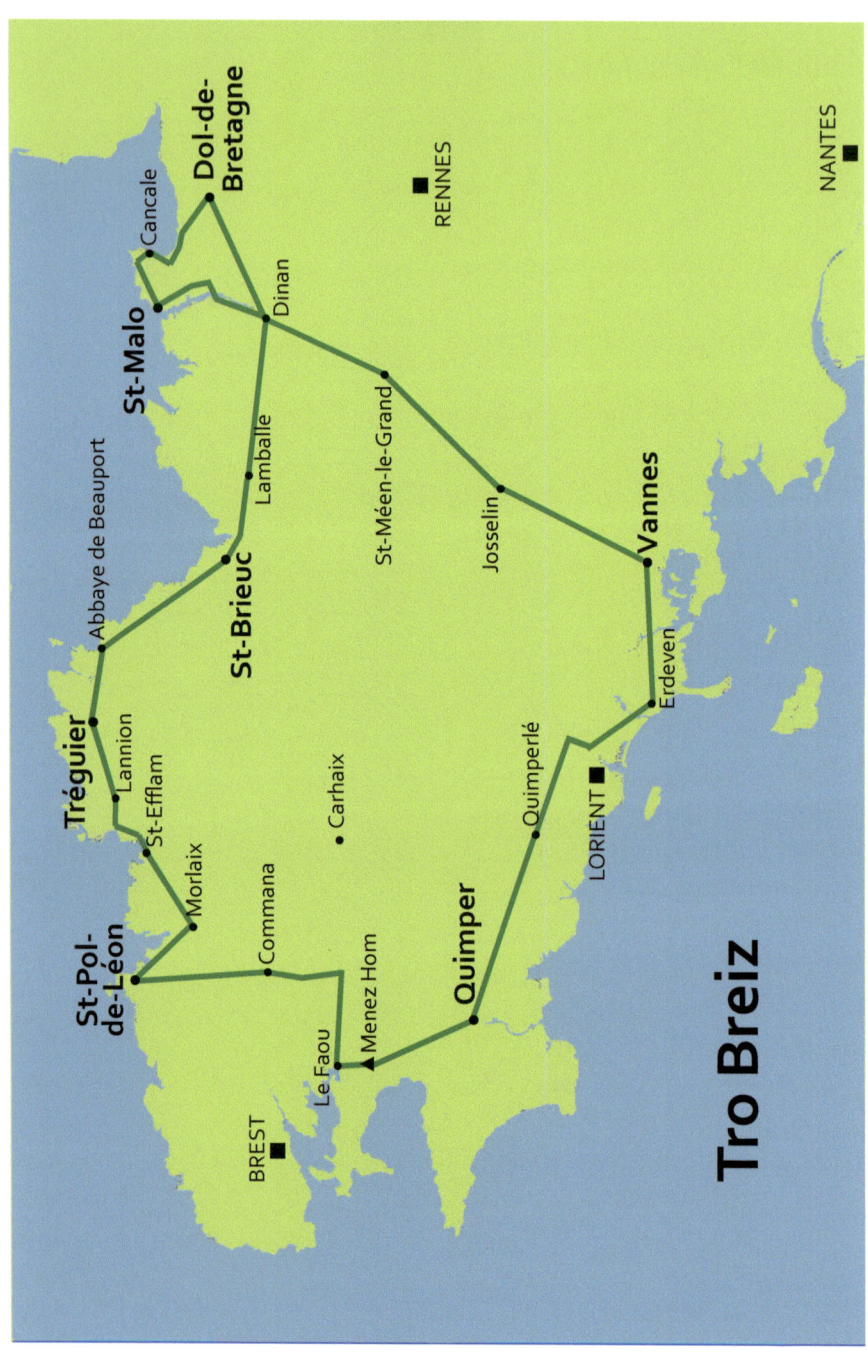

INTRODUCTION

The Tro Breiz is a pilgrimage of indistinct medieval origins. The name means Journey around Brittany, and may also be spelt Tro Breizh in modern Breton language. It links the seven cathedrals of the traditional seven founding saints, who were thought to be at the heart of the origins of western Brittany during the Dark Ages. This was particularly the period of the 6-7th centuries CE, when the land still bore its Roman name Armorica (from land of the sea in Celtic parlance), long before any notion of a unified Breton state emerged. The name *Petite Bretagne* (Little Britain or Brittany) gradually gained usage later on. Historical evidence is fragmentary and inconclusive, but a much later saying claimed that all Bretons must make the journey of the Tro Breiz in their lifetime or face doing the same thing after death at the rate of one coffin length a day.

The seven stages of the Tro Breiz connect the towns (and saints) of Saint-Pol-de-Léon (Saint Pol or Paul Aurelien), Tréguier (Saint Tugdual or Tudwal), Saint-Brieuc (Saint Brieuc), Saint-Malo (Saint Malo), Dol-de-Bretagne (Saint Samson), Vannes (Saint Patern) and Quimper (Saint Corentin). The origins of the seven saints are not a clear matter of historical fact, with most evidence coming from hagiographies written much later and stories from the oral tradition, but perhaps five were from Wales and two were first generation immigrants born in Armorica. These Celtic saints owed their status to popular acclaim rather than official sanction, and today four of the seven cathedrals have official Catholic saints as patrons rather than the original Breton ones. The pilgrimage was called the *Pélerinage des sept saints de Bretagne* (Pilgrimage of the Seven Saints) in its earliest form.

The saints were to become important in notions of Breton identity and heritage in the late 19th century, with their contribution of Celtic roots providing a strong anchor against the perceived buffeting Brittany had received from France since the Revolution. The issue of faith became divisive in the face of active Republican laicity, especially in the years leading to the formal separation of Church and State in 1905. The sense of the Breton saints representing something seminal and enduring in the history and culture of Brittany was fostered then and remains robust today.

The length of the Tro Breiz pilgrimage depends very much on the chosen routes, of which there are many variants, but the basic circuit is a little over 1,000kms. The circular nature of the Tro Breiz is one of its striking features, an uncommon form of sacred journey, like the Shikoku pilgrimage in Japan which visits 88 temples over about 1,200 kilometres around one island. Recent moves have been made to expand the Breton route to make a considerably larger shape including the major cities of Rennes and Nantes, although this somewhat changes the original nature of the pilgrimage as these places were not founded by Breton saints, being part of the Gallo-Roman world rather than from the Celtic tradition.

The idea of reviving this elusive ancient practice for modern experience came most strongly in the 1990s with the establishment of the association Chemins du Tro Breiz (see p.33), which continues today to organise a mass walk each summer covering one stage in one week, with an emphasis on the religious aspect of pilgrimage. Another more recent group, Mon Tro Breizh, the name indicating the very individual nature of such a journey, are in the process of waymarking the whole route and publishing detailed (French) guidebooks with maps of each section. The waymarks are in the colours of the distinctive Breton flag, black and white, with a stylised symbol of the ermine (see p. 35).

The route follows mostly small roads, rural footpaths, the coastal path and Green Ways (*voies vertes*), which are tracks converted from old railway lines or canal towpaths. The medieval route would have followed the lines of existing Roman roads where possible, as these were the only made surfaces available. Walking the Tro Breiz is a wonderful introduction to Brittany's very varied landscape from the lonely moors of the Monts d'Arrée to deep forests like the Forêt de Paimpont, aligned by some with Arthurian Brocéliande, and many beautiful river valleys as well as the unforgettable spectacle of an imposing coastline, particularly in the Bays of Saint Brieuc and Saint Michel. There is also the opportunity to explore historic towns like Morlaix, Pontrieux, Dinan and Josselin, but the rural peace of country villages remains the dominant keynote of the pilgrimage.

Wayside cross   *Waymarking*

Brittany's astonishingly rich cultural heritage is laid out all along the way with megaliths in the form of standing-stones and burial chambers from the neolithic period, chapels, roadside calvaries and sacred springs to mark Christianisation of the landscape, and ruined castles, manor houses and dominant châteaux from many periods of Breton history. There is also much evidence of economic and social history to be discovered, like the cloth industry which brought such prosperity to the areas of Léon and the Trégor in the 17th century. In addition to the splendour of the seven cathedrals, the parishes closes in northern Finistère offer a unique form of Breton tradition and show a region fully in tune with European artistic trends of Gothic, Renaissance and Baroque architecture.

The Tro Breiz is very much more than a religious pilgrimage trail, although that in itself is interesting enough. It offers a chance to discover the whole panorama of Breton history from the Breton saints of the Dark Ages to the emergence of Brittany in the 9th century, the struggle to maintain independence from France, and armed conflicts from the Wars of Religion up to the German Occupation of WWII and the Resistance. Walking the route also provides a close view of diverse local culture, with all its many legends, and the people who shaped the land and customs to create Brittany as we know it today.

PILGRIMAGE

This type of journey connecting sacred sites and with a particular goal at the end has been a feature of many religions of the world for a very long time. It is accompanied by all manner of rituals and devotions for the faithful, such as presenting 'passports' to be stamped at each stage to prove progress along the way, and participation in specific services. The best known in the Catholicism of western Europe are the Camino de Santiago (also known as the Compostela trail or Way of Saint James) to northern Spain and the Via Francigena between Canterbury and Rome. The Hajj and the Umrah are major Muslim pilgrimages to Mecca, and the Shikoku island tour of 88 temples has been a way of reverence for many centuries in Japan. In Brittany there is even a very short form of joint Christian/Muslim pilgrimage in the annual Pardon at Sept Saints in Côtes d'Armor, in honour of the Seven Sleepers of Ephesus, revered by both religions (and without connection to the seven founding saints of the Tro Breiz).

The origins of pilgrimage in Catholicism lay in religious duty, offering a way to do penance for sin and gain indulgences by visiting shrines to make offerings and honour the relics of saints. These relics are said to be anatomical remains such as arm and leg bones, fingers or even skulls, which have traditionally been the source of miracles when touched and prayed over. There was a lucrative medieval trade in relics - which could undermine the notion of authenticity - as churches and chapels vied to house these objects because they would attract visitors and income. The skull of Saint Yves in Tréguier in Brittany, for example, is carried in the Pardon procession each May before being returned to the cathedral (see p.57). It is an object of veneration on the Tro Breiz.

This Breton pilgrimage was thought to take about a month for participants, so in earlier periods the timing of these long journeys depended for some on the rhythm of the farming year. There were four periods in Brittany when the circuit might have been possible for working people: Easter, Whitsun, Michaelmas and Christmas. The weather was obviously a factor and there was also the question of availability of wild food, which was pretty much limited to May to September. Travel during winter was more dangerous and would have required more resources for successful completion, such as the money for lodgings and prepared food. Other hazards at any time were robbers, wolves and unscrupulous landlords providing insalubrious accommodation. Travelling in a group was desirable for such reasons, but it was not always possible. Most of our evidence concerns individuals or a pair of travellers. It was even possible to hire a professional pilgrim to undertake the journey on someone else's behalf.

Tro Breiz depart Dol   *Pardon of St Yves*

There were other more liberating aspects to pilgrimage in these pre-holiday medieval times. They provided a sense of freedom from everyday demands and routine, and offered a degree of social life on the road, as we can see in Chaucer's Canterbury Tales, where a group of pilgrims in 14th century England travel together and entertain each other with very individual stories. Encounters with new people and places offered a broadening of vision for many, and the large towns with their massive stone structures must have been awe-inspiring for rural dwellers who rarely left their own patches of land. There presumably was often an element of pleasure and relaxation, something we take for granted today as a natural part of our holidays, which many of us can experience as and when we want whether on a small local scale or a block of travelling time for sight-seeing and adventure.

Medieval pilgrims were not deliberately travelling what we might regard as scenic routes, such as the coast, but connecting religious points of chapels, churches and cathedrals by the safest and most direct routes. In Brittany this was often on the basis of such Roman roads as still existed regardless of their state of repair. Before the custom officers' paths developed along the coast in the 19th century, this environment may have been more hazardous than inland travel, if demanding terrain of cliffs and coves was involved, but various vast sandy beaches in the large shallow bays of northern Brittany were known to be used as crossing-points for pilgrims (see p.50). In the countryside, villages were connected by a series of paths and sunken ways, hollowed out by driving animals to market, cart-tracks and even coffin roads. Some of these are fortunately still in existence.

Modern pilgrimage retains the religious motivation for many, but now people might commit to these long journeys for a variety of more personal reasons: honouring a lost loved one, seeking time to think through important issues, physical challenge or social stimulation. They are often a catalyst for change on completion, with new directions chosen in everyday life on return. Mental and emotional movement often goes along with the physical journeying.

Since the pandemic of 2021-2, pilgrimage has become increasingly popular as people are able to travel again and seek new, more meaningful experiences. Many are looking for something beyond just a sun-tan, photos and souvenirs to show for their personal excursions. Having a definite goal in terms of distance or reaching a famous shrine also provides motivation. Ritual along the way – religious, spiritual or purely personal – can add a sense of profundity and achievement, giving a lasting feeling of growth and progression in individual lives.

The Tro Breiz offers the opportunity for all these experiences, whatever the motivation, timescale or physical abilities. People undergo the journey at any time of year, although there may be limitations for transport and accommodation in winter. It can be undertaken on foot, by bike, car or even train with the help of a few taxis! Both men and women choose to walk alone or with a companion or in a small group of friends.

There is a chance to join a Catholic mass walk with like-minded spirits once a year (see p. 33), joining hundreds of others on a religious exploration of one section of the Tro Breiz. This experience of '*communitas*', stepping outside one's norms and mixing with all sorts of people regardless of age, gender or social status, is often the motive for seekers. Some take the time out to walk the whole pilgrimage in one go, but there is plenty of scope for going at it more slowly, perhaps one stage at a time even over a number of years. Why not? There is no hurry. Brittany is always there and ready with deep layers for exploration.

SOME RELEVANT RELIGIOUS BACKGROUND

Christianity and paganism

Before the arrival of Christianity in western Brittany, pagan religious practices were nature based, with, for example, neolithic megaliths, springs and remarkable trees regarded as sacred and animate. The Druids were the priests of the Celtic tribes occupying the west of what was then called Armorica. The Church of Rome, as it grew, took various stances on such things in the countries where it had spread. Early Christian edicts (at Arles in 452, for example) were issued by popes against pagan shrines and the cult of stones, and many were destroyed. Later on, assimilation was regarded as a more productive policy and the Christianisation of many sites began. Pope Gregory I advocated eradicating pagan idols, but re-using pagan places of worship to win people over to the Christian faith. Popular traditions and superstitions alike persisted through the centuries, however, mixing and mingling with Christian stories and symbolism, a fusion that seemed acceptable to the populace in Brittany even if the church rallied against it from time to time.

The Venus of Quinipily (near Baud in Morbihan), a large statue of a pagan goddess, became a target of the wrath of the Bishop of Vannes in 1661, because locals made her the centre of worship on a hill in Castennec. He persuaded the nobleman there to have the statue destroyed but people rushed to defend their goddess. She was eventually thrown into the Blavet river, but when torrential rains destroyed the harvest as if in retribution, the statue was fished out and resurrected. Four years later, it was flung back into the water. After the nobleman suffered a terrible fall from his horse, the Venus rose once again from the river and was installed where she now stands in the garden of the former château of Quinipily. These events well illustrate the abiding amalgam of local tradition, which has a wider interpretation of 'religion', and the Catholic Church. For ordinary people, especially in the countryside where livelihoods clearly depended on weather and natural processes, there was room for both in their lives, with an enduring history of harvest festivals and seasonal celebrations that long pre-dated Christianity.

Viking attacks

The nascent state of Brittany came under frequent attack from different groups of Viking raiders in the 9th and 10th centuries. This period saw much devastation, particularly on the coast and in areas accessible by navigable rivers. Many abbeys and churches were sacked, such as Landévennec on the Rade de Brest in 913. Fortunately, the monks had time to remove themselves and their valuables, unlike Bishop Gohard of Nantes who was slaughtered at the cathedral altar in 843 in a surprise assault. All over Brittany monks (and nobles) departed from the territory to safer regions in France, taking with them manuscripts and saints' relics, many of which never returned. Reconstruction of religious buildings had to wait until the violence was over. Alain Barbetorte achieved a notable victory over the invaders near Dol-de-Bretagne in 939 and gradually the raids ceased as the bands of Vikings either departed or settled.

Crusades and pilgrimage

Pilgrimage to the Holy Land had existed since the 3rd century CE with Christians seeking to put themselves in the locations of the life of Christ. The Crusades to oust the Muslims from Jerusalem began with the call of Pope Urban II in the late 11th century. They were in essence armed pilgrimages (the Latin word for pilgrimage, *peregrinatio,* was used in this context) with a specific goal. The practice of religious journeys began to gain greater significance from this time (although by no means restricted to Christianity).

The Paix de Dieu (Peace of God) movement, initiated by the church and supported by the king of France, was designed to restore peace and stability after the turmoil of warring centuries. One of their decrees was to protect pilgrims on religious journeys and guarantee their safety, with penalties for infringement. This was also the period when the Compostela trail to Spain began its rise in popularity. Orders like the Knights Templar and the Knights Hospitaller (Order of Saint John) came into existence to protect the interests of pilgrims travelling to the eastern Mediterranean. Both these organisations were to have a later presence in Brittany, still echoed on the Tro Breiz route today.

Reformation and Counter-Reformation

The Protestant Reformation ultimately stemmed from Martin Luther's declaration of 95 Theses in 1517, decrying the corruption of the church especially in the granting of indulgences (remission of sin) for money. Other abuses such as the trade in saints' relics (often of dubious authenticity) and even the adulation of the saints and their acclaimed miracles turned many from the Church of Rome and fanned the beginning of the Protestant faith. France generally and Brittany in particular remained staunchly Catholic, with some exceptions among the nobility (see below).

The Catholic Counter-Reformation (Council of Trent, 1545-1563), an attempt at reform of the worst excesses with a recall to the essentials of the faith, also placed an increasing emphasis on religious fervour and the emotional engagement of worshippers. The Holy Family and especially Marian devotions proliferated from this time. Mary as Our Lady (Notre Dame) has a statue or shrine in most Breton churches today. Often traditional (non-Breton) Catholic saints were installed as patrons of churches and chapels, with the many hundreds of Breton saints from the Dark Ages regarded by officialdom as little more than illiterate superstition. The ordinary people, however, never lost their attachment to these pioneers of their early communities, and saints were often the focus of local identity.

Wars of Religion

The new polarisation of different versions of Christianity, Catholics and Protestants (Huguenots), led to the Wars of Religion in France from 1562-1598. The Catholic League was an alliance of French nobles determined to stamp out Protestantism. Henri de Bourbon, first king of Navarre who became King Henri IV of France from 1589, was baptised a Catholic but brought up a Protestant. He renounced this faith in 1572 but returned to it in 1576, something that was to be a great issue when he inherited the French throne against the wishes of the majority of Catholic nobles.

This complicated struggle was contested all over staunchly Catholic Brittany with great loss of life and much destruction. It was a severe deterrent to travel, such as pilgrimages, in the countryside, and may have halted regular passage on the Tro Breiz. Catholics were in a strong numerical majority, although a few of the greatest nobles in the land, like the Rohan and Laval families, were Protestants. The wars ended with the Edict of Nantes (1598) in which the French king granted religious tolerance for Protestants, and Pope Clement VIII reluctantly accepted it.

Missionaries in Brittany

The 16/17th century was a time of religious flowering in Brittany, from the construction of churches and chapels with lavish attention to artistic (often Baroque) detail, to a proliferation of religious orders establishing convents and seminaries for the training of priests. The Jesuits were especially active in the field of education. It was also the setting for a series of missions to the parishes in the west to revitalise understanding and adherence to basic tenets of the Church.

Missionaries Michel Le Nobletz and his successor Julien Maunoir travelled widely, using both simple visual aids like painted animal skins (*taolennoù*) and fiery words to remind people of the need for salvation through the teachings of the Church and the life of Jesus Christ. Maunoir, who was born in eastern Brittany at Fougères and therefore did not speak Breton, had to learn the local language to make headway with the people in the west (see p.24). He produced a collection of Breton canticles, including a 'Prayer in honour of the Seven Saints of Brittany'.

The elaborate stone calvaries of many parish closes (see p.147) performed the same function, reinforcing the message of the Gospels in pictorial form. The inevitability of Death was a theme omnipresent in Breton religious life, with Ankou, the Grim Reaper, and scenes of hellish punishments appearing graphically in religious art and architecture as a stern reminder of the only way to salvation.

It was also in this period (1637) that an immensely influential book, *La vie, gestes, mort et miracles des Saincts de la Bretaigne Armorique* (The Life, Deeds, Death and Miracles of the Saints of Armorican Brittany) was published. It contained the lives of 78 saints, in hagiographical style. The author Albert le Grand was a Dominican monk from Morlaix. Drawing on both legendary and historical sources, the book was a huge success and re-drew attention to the cults of saints.

French Revolution

The triumph of Republicanism in the Revolution saw savage suppression of religion. Cathedrals were looted and sacked. Statues that had not been hidden by the faithful were decapitated and destroyed, with a determined hostility towards the saints and anything deemed 'superstitious'. The cult of Reason was established in the main towns: in Quimper a temple to this abstract goddess was set up on the opposite bank of the Odet from the cathedral.

Priests were forced to take an oath of first allegiance to the civil constitution, putting the state before God. In the west, especially in Léon, up to 90% of priests refused to sign. Many went into exile and many were hidden by their loyal parishioners, especially in rural communities, as Republicanism was significantly an urban phenomenon. Some even blessed the guns of the Chouans who fought to save their priests. These Catholic, anti-Revolutionary royalists operated armed bands all over Brittany to defend their churches and traditional way of life.

The fighting gradually died down with Napoleon's rise to power and his signature of the Concordat in 1801 with Pope Pius VII. This allowed religious practices to resume and many cult buildings were restored to the Church, but it also required bishops and priests to swear fidelity to the government. Rather than the religion of the state, Catholicism was declared only as the religion of the majority.

Tensions in 19th century

Throughout the 19th century there were growing tensions between Catholic traditionalists (Whites) and Republican progressives (Blues). In local political terms there was often conflict between these two groups and their relative influences, over education in particular. Léon (northern Finistère) was known as 'the land of priests' for the tight grip of the Church over social behaviour and family life. Rural communities everywhere remained tenacious of traditional practices. In the final years of the century, the diametrically opposed factions can best be illustrated by events in Tréguier (see p.56), where a statue of the goddess of Reason, Athena, was provocatively placed outside the cathedral, together with that of local philosopher Ernest Renan.

These struggles, taking place all over France, led to the formal separation of Church and State in 1905.

THE BRETON SAINTS

In the period after the fall of the Roman Empire often called the Dark Ages, waves of migration from Great Britain brought many holy men (and a few women) across the Channel to mainly western Armorica. Most probably came from monasteries in Wales (like Llanwit Major) via Cornwall to avoid a long sea journey. The two shores had known commercial connection at least since the Bronze Age. Now there was Anglo-Saxon and Pictish aggression to cope with in Britain and pressures on the availability of workable land may also have been a factor in certain areas.

Some migrants came alone, others with groups of supporters from the conventional number of 12 (like the apostles) to perhaps as many as a hundred. Their aim was to evangelise the scantily populated land that awaited, primarily in the west of the peninsula and along the north coast where they first arrived. This process was not an orchestrated movement but a piecemeal phenomenon continued over several hundred years, with the 6-7th centuries a peak time for arrivals. The monks were to set up establishments in their adopted territory, from simple oratories and churches to monasteries which would soon become the hub of new communities.

Many of these monks were from aristocratic backgrounds, choosing the monastic life of prayer and teaching rather than having political or military ambitions. After training in British monasteries they were sent or chose to go across the Channel. Their motivation for the journey to Armorica with all its attendant risks was basically to spread the word of God to godless places, but on reaching the empty countryside, some were attracted to the prospect of a life of prayer and devotion in peaceful isolation. (The notion of asceticism was strong in the Celtic tradition.) Saint Pol was one such, but the vision of an angel drove him on each time he was tempted to stop, as he was destined for much greater things than obscurity. Others found they already knew earlier settlers from Great Britain and had ready-made contacts to help them on arrival.

The west of Armorica was sparsely populated, an area little touched by Roman rule of north-west France, although there are a few remains from that period. The Roman roads, often based on earlier trading routes, but better made, would have been useful for travelling. There is also evidence of buried coin hoards for people abandoning their native places in the turbulent times of coastal raids and the political vacuum which followed Roman withdrawal. Small well-spaced communities with individual rulers controlling their immediate environment and fighting when necessary to protect or expand their resources was the order of the day. There was plenty of space for development and the growth of towns or villages around the new monasteries, which could be exploited by the incomers, once local patronage had been obtained.

Eastern areas of the peninsula that would become Brittany or Little Britain had evolved rather differently, with greater Roman influence and considerable religious development. Rennes and Nantes were already established towns and had their own churches and church organisation with appointed bishops under the jurisdiction of the Pope in Rome. So Christianity was well-developed and formalised here, unlike in the wilder west where the incoming monks from Great Britain are often said to have practised 'Celtic Christianity'. This is a controversial subject, but an interesting letter from the early 6th century survives, with bishops from Angers, Tours and Rennes urging two of their brethren in the west of Brittany to desist from practices such as taking the sacrament from house to house with a portable altar, and allowing women to participate in administering the mass. This suggests a less formal nature for the early Christian communities set up by the British migrants.

Conflicting ideas can be seen even in the practical issue of the hairstyles of monks, with the Celtic (Druid-like) version (front half of the head shaved, rest of the hair left long) and the Church of Rome's preference for the tonsure (leaving only a ring of hair around the crown). Louis the Pious, emperor of the Franks 814-840, was in Brittany in person early in his reign to try to enforce control over the Bretons. After defeating the powerful chieftain Morvan, he summoned the Abbot of Landévennec to a meeting and insisted that such Celtic customs should be abandoned in his abbey and the rules of Benedictine establishments strictly applied. This was diplomatically accepted, but it seems that these instructions were not consistently obeyed in subsequent years.

The Breton churches were to be further encouraged in their independence in the mid-9th century by the actions of Nominoë, a noble of western Brittany appointed by Louis to keep the region in order and put an end to incursions into the Franks' territory. After Louis' death, he forged a relatively united force set on pushing out the boundaries of a developing Breton state. Religion was as much a part of Nominoë's plan for strengthening Brittany as political and military moves. The focus of this ambition was to be the promotion of the see of Dol-de-Bretagne (where the first bishop Samson was one of the founding saints in the 6th century), and a challenge to the Rome-given authority of the archbishop of Tours (see p.95) over the Breton bishops. It was a rivalry that was to run for centuries.

We know about the lives of the Breton saints mainly from later hagiographies that mostly present them in the fashion of the genre as supreme examples of Christian behaviour, miracle-workers and healers. Some details in these accounts hint at hostile receptions for some of the arrivals: not all were welcomed with open arms. This is hardly surprising as threats to territory and resources could be seen as a challenge to the power of native rulers.

Saint Ké was beaten by women with twigs of gorse until he fell bleeding to the ground and needed the waters of a miraculously appearing spring to revive him. Saint Ronan, who did not have a personality designed to ingratiate himself, was chased away from the coast where he landed in the Bay of Douarnenez as he immediately accused the locals of being wreckers. He fled inland to the place now called Locronan, the holy place of Ronan. Overall, however, there seems to have been a positive reception for the representatives of the new religion and the abilities they demonstrated. Many Britons were already established in western Armorica and incomers might even find themselves among relatives.

The legendary aspect of the Breton saints was apparent from the first as many were said to have arrived in stone boats, a remarkable feat in itself, suggesting exceptional powers deriving from their Christian god. It gives their appearance in their new land a touch of the miraculous. The stories may have arisen later from the appearance of boat-shaped rocks on the many beaches of Brittany or even from a confusion between the Latin word *cumba* (little boat) and the Breton *koum* (valley shape, so stone trough). Some said that the saints brought their own altar stones with them on the sea journey and these have also made their way into some legends. Several saints went overboard in bad conditions and were said to have used their portable altars as floats to reach land. The simple boats of the day made from wood and skins, which were perfectly capable of transferring passengers across the Channel in about 24 hours, would often have carried stones for cooking hearths or simply ballast to be jettisoned in a storm.

On arrival the holy men had to find suitable locations to settle and establish good relations with the locals. Their first actions were often compelling demonstrations of miracles and healing. Tapping the earth to bring forth a spring was a common feat, and curing the relatives of native lords was certainly a move likely to be rewarded with a place to build a monastic community. Even those who arrived alone and set up life in a cave or basic hermitage often attracted visitors through curiosity linked to their reputations as healers and teachers. Another story told of many saints was the triumph over wild animals, which symbolised the waning power of paganism and the old animistic Celtic religion, led by the Druids. Marauding beasts like dragons which had been eating people and destroying crops were tamed and persuaded to hurl themselves off cliffs into the sea. Wolves, a realistic danger at the time, were said to bow down before the sign of the cross made by a saint and were forced to work in place of domestic animals they had killed. All these acts demonstrated the powers of the new god working through the saints and encouraged conversions to Christianity.

St Samson. St Conogan's boat

A modern **stone boat** was sculpted from granite in 2002 by Jean-Yves Menez. The project took two years, with the resulting vessel 4m long and 1,85m wide. And it floats! The Maen Vag (stone boat in Breton) has undertaken numerous voyages, carrying up to 20 people. It currently rests outside the west door of the cathedral in Dol-de-Bretagne.

In addition to the word of Christianity, the incomers also brought their language, which would eventually form Breton, together with local influences. Breton is closest to Cornish and Welsh, indicating the saints' origins, and native speakers of these languages have little difficulty in communicating with each other today. Looking at place-names in the areas the saints colonised shows a proliferation of the prefix *Plou* (= parish), often followed by the name of a saint: Plounéour means the parish of Saint Enéour. *Gui(k)* is the same, as in the village name Guimiliau (Saint Miliau). *Loc* and *Lan(n)* indicate holy places of a saint, such as Locmalo, Lannedern, Locmelar. Many Breton saints were second generation immigrants, like Saint Guénolé who was the son of Fragan who had earlier settled where Ploufragan is today. There was no tradition of Breton-speaking later in areas untouched by the arrival of the saints. Eastern Brittany had its own language, Gallo, derived from vulgar Latin.

It is important to note that the Breton saints were not officially accepted as such by the Catholic Church. (Far from it, as the patronage of many cathedrals, churches and chapels has been transferred from their original Breton founders to traditional Catholic favourites, like Saint Laurent and Saint Vincent Ferrier, whose shrines might be found in many other regions.) They were saints by popular and local acclaim, for the example of their devout conduct and the exceptional powers they demonstrated when alive or through relics (bones) after their deaths. Most died peacefully in their beds surrounded by supporters, unlike the early Christian martyrs who were made official saints after suffering terrible torture for their faith in Europe or the Holy Land.

Brittany does have two official saints in the later medieval period, firstly in Guillaume Pinchon, bishop of Saint Brieuc who died in 1234 and was canonised thirteen years later. Much more famously, Saint Yves of Tréguier (d.1303) followed a hundred years later, after a long process of enquiry into miracles attested at his tomb in the cathedral. He became the male patron saint of the region, whilst Saint Anne, mother of the Virgin Mary and known only from the Apocrypha, became his female equivalent (see p.142). This pairing well-illustrates the paradox of historically documented individuals like Saint Yves and a semi-legendary figure such as Anne, equally revered in the world of Breton saints.

The importance of the Breton saints remains to this day in the hearts and minds of Breton communities, and continues to foster the pride of local identity. The annual Pardon or celebration of the individual saints' special days is a meaningful tradition still celebrated in many towns and villages. Some of these events attract thousands, others only a handful, but they all echo a profound and lasting attachment to the heritage of the saints, reaching back to the very origins of Brittany.

SACRED SEVEN: THE FOUNDING SAINTS

Of the hundreds of Breton saints, seven (a sacred number in many biblical contexts) emerged in traditional estimation as the founders of Brittany. This title reflects their role as the original bishops to be established from the migrant movement and the impact they made as leaders on local church development. They set up the layers of religious organisation which gave form and structure to the early Church in the peninsula. Their settlements also became the basis of many towns and villages still in existence today. One of the saints, Samson, had considerable political influence in the wider world. Their reputations also rested on the exceptional virtue and miraculous powers which they demonstrated in their lives, and after death through their tombs and relics.

Although we speak of their 'cathedrals' forming the links of the Tro Breiz pilgrimage, it is worth remembering that in those early times of the saints, construction was essentially of wood, and nothing of this type survived the savage Viking raids and incursions of the 9th century. Building in stone on a large scale began from the 12th century, and the cathedrals we know today on the sites of earlier structures were mostly developed in the 13-15th centuries. How extraordinary these constructions must have seemed to medieval pilgrims!

Although the essence may have taken root in the time of Nominoë (see p.22), the notion of seven founding saints seems to have been consolidated in the 11/12th centuries. There may have been both political and religious motivations, creating an image of the early origins of Brittany as a Celtic state to emphasise the difference from France and the French. It was part of the concept of national identity that has always been so important in Brittany. As the writing of hagiographies (the Lives of Saints) flourished in this period, the tradition of the seven founding saints really began to take hold.

Saint Corentin, who reluctantly became the first bishop of Quimper, may have been a first generation immigrant. He lived in the 5th century as a hermit at the foot of Menez Hom (in what is now called Finistère). For survival he had struck the ground to produce a stream of water with a little pool which contained a single fish. Each day Corentin caught the fish, cut off a slice and threw it back. Each time it regenerated, providing an endless source of nourishment for the hermit. One day he was discovered by the hunting party of Gradlon, a king in the process of establishing a new power base, which was to be the town of Quimper. He was so impressed by Corentin and the miraculous fish that he insisted on making the hermit bishop of a new 'cathedral' and giving him an important role as regal advisor. The fish is Corentin's icon in statuary (see p.34) and his story can be seen in the stained glass window of his chapel in Quimper cathedral.

This notion of the reluctant bishop is replayed in the story of **Saint Pol**. He arrived from Wales firstly on the island of Ouessant and then made his way across northern Finistère with his followers to the site of his future 'cathedral' at what is now Saint-Pol-de-Léon. His own instinct was for a quiet life of prayer on the Île de Batz, but the local lord Withur had other ideas, keen to exploit the miraculous powers of the saint. Once Pol had dealt with a ravening dragon (which became his icon) on the island, he came under great pressure to take up an official position in the new town developing on the mainland.

Withur had to resort to trickery to make him a bishop and this ensured a public role for the reluctant saint. Even in old age when Pol tried to retire, he was called back to episcopal life and the peace he craved was ever hard to find. Another slant, however, shows him a vigorous organiser and promoter of Christianity.

Saint Tugdual (or more correctly Tudwal) is also called Pabu or Babu (father) in reference to the legend that he went to Rome for a visit during the ceremony to choose a new pope. He was unexpectedly appointed to the post after the omen of a dove landing on his shoulder, and this became his symbol in statuary. He later had a miraculous return to Brittany from Italy on a flying horse in a single night's journey. In some versions he arrives on the continent as part of Saint Brieuc's party, whereas in others he lands at Le Conquet and travels east; founding a monastery at what is now Trebabu, to the spot where his 'cathedral' would be established at Tréguier in about 535 CE. He may have been the nephew of Riwal, lord of Domnonée who had arrived in Armorica many years earlier, but Tugdual remains a rather shadowy figure.

Construction   Seven saints (Kreisker chapel)

The town of Saint Brieuc was said to have developed from the monastery founded by **Saint Brieuc** c485. He had arrived in Armorica with 80 followers in the valley of the Gouët river and started to exploit land nearby for a settlement when soldiers intervened and took him before the local ruler (who turned out to be his cousin). Riwal had in fact been struck by pain and paralysis after giving the order to seize the newcomers. After mutual recognition, Brieuc was able to heal his kinsman of all affliction, thus demonstrating his exceptional powers and the validity of his deity. The site of his first simple oratory is preserved by an ornamental *fontaine* (sacred spring) in Saint Brieuc today (see p.67). His icon is a pair or group of wolves following the story that, after an attack on his travelling party, he tamed them with the sign of the cross, symbolising the conversion of pagans to Christianity.

Saint Malo or Maclou (6th-7th century) was from Wales and participated in the legendary voyage of Saint Brendan. His iconography of a whale recalls the story of stopping on what was apparently an island but turned out to be the back of this huge mammal. Malo then settled for a time on a small island with the hermit Aaron, before moving to the mainland opposite at Aleth (now Saint Servan today) where he became bishop of a new foundation. (The site of the 'cathedral' was later moved to where the walled city of Saint Malo is today, see p.82.) The saint unfortunately fell out with his followers and excommunicated them all before fleeing the town, returning only briefly later from Charente to lift the ban.

The most influential of all the saints was **Saint Samson**, who founded his settlement at what is now Dol-de-Bretagne, after being given land as a reward for acts of healing. He seems to have been a natural leader, and we know from an historical document that he participated in the Council of Paris in c560. The first hagiography of Samson, probably written in the 7th or 8th century, is the earliest such evidence for the migration of the saints. He also had connections at the court of the king of the Franks, Childebert, and managed to persuade this great political figure to release the Breton chief Judual who was living under a sort of house arrest in Paris. This restraint of a rival was at the behest of the warlord Conomor who was seeking to expand his power in Brittany by any means possible. The bishopric of Dol-de-Bretagne was to play a crucial role in the development of Brittany in the 9th century (see p.95).

Perhaps the least known of the founding saints is **Saint Patern**, who became bishop of Vannes. Some odd stories attach to his character, including a brush with King Arthur, who coveted a fine cloak Patern had acquired in the Holy Land, and details of his life are obscure, perhaps sometimes confused with that of Paterne, bishop of Avranches. One story has his parents separate in Armorica, and Patern later follow his father to Great Britain where he founded monasteries before returning to the continent. There is also the mysterious quarrel with his parishioners much later, which led to Patern fleeing Brittany into France and eventually dying there. As a result, Vannes suffered many punishments until a new church, separate to the cathedral, was established in Patern's honour, just outside the walls, where a later version stands today.

EVIDENCE

Our knowledge of the historic Tro Breiz is fragmentary and does not add up to a coherent picture of the pilgrimage, but the religious and cultural importance of the founding saints is plain. All seven were dead by 650CE, but clearly not forgotten. The earliest evidence consists of references to the Seven Saints of Brittany in 11th century documents. The Song of Roland, a famous *chanson de geste*, refers to a banner with this inscription (*VII. Sains de Bretaingne*) and from a

See p. 30-31

Manuscript

similar period, the missal of Vougay in Finistère includes a prayer to the seven founding saints of Brittany. This seems to be the time when this group of seven emerged as an emblematic entity, although clear definition remains elusive.

The traditional seven saints are actually named in a 12th century manuscript which appears to be a Life of the Irish Saint Ronan. A scribe has added a cartouche with the words *Homma VII Scot 7 britannie* (Scotti means Irish, but may also have the more general connotation of Celtic), followed by the seven names Brioci (Brieuc), Samson, Machut (Malo), Patern, Corentin, Pol, Tugdual. Here the reference is specific, but a problem with other references to the Seven Saints is that they are not always actually named individually, and we know from testamentary evidence, for example, that sometimes the list was different. (There are also other unrelated groups of saints, such as the Seven Sleepers of Ephesus, who are honoured in Brittany at Vieux-Marché in Côtes d'Armor, see page 10.)

In the 13th century, Guillaume Le Borgne, senechal of Goëlo, left a hundred pounds to be shared between the abbeys of Brittany and the churches of the Seven Saints. Nicolas Coatanlem, in his will of 1518, speaks of the journey of the Sept Saints, giving money to each one, but his list includes Saint Pierre of Nantes and Guillaume of Saint Brieuc, leaving out Patern and Corentin.

In the early 18th century, the monk historian Dom Lobineau gave the seven as Saints Paul, Tugdual, Samson, Malo, Meen, Judicael and Corentin.

Historian Pierre Le Baud (d.1505) has some tantalising details that may reflect a contemporary notion of the Tro Breiz. He mentions a 'circuit called the tour of Brittany' (origin of the name) in the context of the episcopal divisions of the time, and in one reference he says specifically that Saint Patern was one of the Seven Saints of Brittany. (He regards Patern and Corentin as natives of the peninsula.) Elsewhere it is noted that Tugdual merits his place in that list by virtue of his miracles, curing the blind and paralytics 'by the mercy of God'.

Some images of the sacred seven as we know them are also to be found in medieval books. In his *Grandes Croniques de Bretaigne* (1514), the historian Alain Bouchart included an illustration of the seven bishops, Samson with his archbishop's cross (see p.29) and the others (except Patern) turned towards him. In the cathedral of Dol-de-Bretagne, the earliest stained glass window in Brittany (13th century) above the main altar has a tiny vignette of what appears to be the traditional saints grouped together around Samson.

The question of the pilgrimage around the seven cathedrals is equally hard to pin down. There are references in the witness statements in the canonisation process of Saint Yves in the 14th century.

Two women from Lanmeur were on the pilgrimage route of the Sept Saints (in 1299) and met Saint Yves on the route between Tréguier and Lannion in the period of Pentecost. Another said that the saint had greased the sandals of a man when he heard he was on the pilgrimage. Duke Jean V is said to have made the journey (in response to a severe attack of measles) with a single companion in the early 15th century. It is worth noting that there is no evidence of organised groups of pilgrims travelling this pilgrimage at this time.

Anne de Bretagne, twice Queen of France and Duchess of Brittany, is said to have carried out the Tro Breiz in 1505 (or 6) but it was not in the strict sense of targeting the seven cathedrals and we do not have the full details of her route. Her avowed motivation was to seek healing for her husband's health (Louis XII, king of France) and she visited many major religious sanctuaries such as Saint-Jean-du-Doigt and Le Folgoët in Finistere, bestowing favours and largesse, as well as the cathedral towns of Vannes, Quimper and Saint-Pol-de-Léon. But the journey was in essence a political progress around her territory, an important tool for rulers presenting themselves directly to the people. She certainly had a huge audience as she passed through the countryside, and much of the legendary tradition about the duchess doubtless originated from the brief glimpses her subjects received at that time.

Another aspect of evidence can be found in the offerings at various shrines as people paid homage to relics of the saints, a major motivation for the sacred journey. Cathedrals may have records of pilgrim donations – Quimper had a special donation box for pilgrims in the 13th century - but it is impossible to know whether the pilgrims were honouring one saint or making a full tour of the region, and if they were on the Tro Breiz route or perhaps that of Saint Jacques de Compostelle. There is no definitive indication of numbers either, even if a claim is made for the sanctuary of Saint Patern in Vannes to have seen about 20,000 pilgrims in a year.

All these examples give a sense of the small glimpses of the Tro Breiz that historical evidence offers in the medieval period when it was at its height. Some commentators infer more from these than others. It seems that pilgrimage in general was less popular by the 17th century, especially after the horrors and disruption of the Wars of Religion. Louis XIV actually passed measures against pilgrimage as people were taking too much time away from their work to follow the trails! Later, the post-French Revolution conflict between Republicans and Chouans, which played out bloodily in many parts of the countryside, would have been a powerful deterrent to religious journeys. Some major works about religion and the saints in Brittany written after the medieval period, make no mention whatsoever of the Tro Breiz pilgrimage.

One example of the practice in the first part of the early 19th century, however, comes from the work of the great folklorist Anatole Le Braz. In *Le Temps Passé* (1901), he records the story told by an elderly rope-maker called Roparz. The old man says he was told as a child about a Green Route, which led to heaven. It was actually part of the Tro Breiz, a sacred way (probably the paved section of Roman road) maintained by locals for pilgrims to follow. Roparz describes how a woman 'Nanna Tro Breiz' stayed with the family every year when he was little. He recalls the thin, wrinkled woman sitting by their fire smoking a little pipe. The woman was a bit of a mystery to the family, but she undertook the Tro Breiz pilgrimage every year, and did so during the winter! Until one year she simply failed to appear. Her real name was Marcharit Fulup (Marguerite Philippe in French), a professional pilgrim and story-teller, whose statue stands near the church in Pluzunet.

It is clear that the Tro Breiz was not entirely lost to memory, and attempts at revival came in the late 19th century with the renaissance of interest in Breton heritage and identity. The use of a Breton name for the journey (Tro Breiz) seems to have come from this time, as the matter of language was crucial, with the persecution of Breton by state authorities. The concept of the founding saints, with their Celtic origins, was an important link with the days of an independent Brittany not yet under the power of the French, so the distinctive inception and pattern of the Tro Breiz fitted well with the development of ideas of Breton nationalism.

It is by both a conceptual and an historical path that the Tro Breiz has assumed its character today, even if it was the 1990s before this pilgrimage really made a contemporary mark on the religious and cultural map of Brittany.

MODERN REVIVAL

The Tro Breiz was revived in the 1990s by an association **Chemins du Tro Breiz**. It continues to this day with a well-attended annual week of pilgrimage covering one of the seven stages of the traditional tour of Brittany. They have now added Rennes and Nantes, however, to expand the scope and distance considerably. (Perhaps this is not surprising in the light of current debates about whether Nantes, which was once a part of Brittany, should be reunited politically with the region.)

The result of all their work has been the development of the route, with alternatives to cover more religious sites such as chapels and sacred springs. Emphasis is on the Catholic/spiritual aspect of the Tro Breiz, with services and prayers along the way on the main summer event, when hundreds of people come together to share this enriching experience. For many, it is the highlight of the year.

For details of their work and membership, see the website **trobreiz.bzh**

A new organisation **Mon Tro Breizh**, has focused on waymarking a definitive route with their distinctive black and white logo (see front cover), and the publication of guidebooks (in French) with general maps to help contemporary walkers to follow the pilgrimage at their own pace. The books do not include written directions, but they offer a choice of the major route and a shorter version where practicable.

Their goal is to encourage people of all ages, with or without spiritual inclination, to explore the culture and heritage of Brittany through the structure of the Tro Breiz. They are in sympathy with the modern fluid interpretation of pilgrimage as anything the individual wants, from a very long walk to a personal challenge or simply an up-close examination of the many wonders Brittany has to offer. Religious heritage is given an emphasis, but the range of reference is much wider.

For details of their work and membership, see the website **montrobreizh.bzh**

The indefatigable **Yvon Autret**, an expert not only of the Tro Breiz but also Roman roads in Brittany, has produced very specific detail of directions (in French) for the pilgrimage, stage by stage, with large scale maps. These can be ordered as individual booklets for each of

Valley of the Saints

2008 saw the start of an astonishing project to bring to life the traditional number of a thousand Breton saints in the form of a statue park. The Vallée des Saints has attracted much attention to this vital part of Breton heritage. A beautiful hillside near Carnoët is gradually being peopled by huge stone statues of historical and legendary figures, with the seven founding saints enjoying pride of place on the summit, a former feudal motte. This outdoor exhibition is also a showcase for the working of Breton granite. In the valley below, the church of Saint Gildas is a very fine example of an older artistic and cultural tradition.

For details: lavalleedessaints.com

Saint Corentin and fish

the seven sections. This information is regularly updated, so as accurate as possible. The directions are given in great detail but sites are not actually marked on the maps.

For details of his work and to buy any of the stage guides, see the website **tro.bzh**

Out of print but still sometimes available second-hand on the internet is **Le Guide du Tro Breiz** (Association Les Chemins du Tro-Breiz and Bernard Rio). This divides the pilgrimage into 47 stages and takes a fairly direct route between the cathedral towns, often using small roads. It includes maps and directions, and information about churches and chapels. Important to note that a few of the paths have changed or are no longer viable, as this guide is more than 10 years old, but it remains a very useful planning tool for those organising their own journey.

Breton flags

The Gwenn ha du (black and white) has nine stripes to represent the historic territories of Brittany, the five black for the Gallo speaking areas with cathedrals at Rennes, Nantes, Dol-de-Bretagne, Saint Malo and Saint Brieuc, with four white for the Breton-speaking territories of Quimper, Saint-Pol-Léon, Tréguier and Vannes. The stylised ermines represent the duchy of Brittany, lost to French control in 1488 at the Battle of Saint-Aubin-du-Cormier. The flag, which has become the modern symbol of Brittany, is only a hundred years old, the creation in 1923 of Morvan Marchal, an architect and prominent member of the Breton Regionalist Union.

An earlier flag representing Brittany is the Kroaz du, a simple black cross on a white background. It may date back to the late 12th century and the Third Crusade, but is clearly attested in a 15th century manuscript illustration of the Battle of the Thirty (1351) a staged contest during the Wars of Succession. Corresponding to the nine bishoprics, the nine historic districts of Brittany - Cornouaille (Quimper), Léon (St-Pol), Trégor (Tréguier), Broërec (Vannes), Dol, Saint Brieuc, Saint Malo (see photo above), Nantes and Rennes each had their own flag and many of these are carried in the annual Tro Breiz marches (see p.98) to represent pilgrims from those individual territories.

Kreisker Chapel

SAINT-POL-de-LÉON

The cathedral town of Saint-Pol-de-Léon, very close to Roscoff, is said to have been founded in the 6th century when Saint Pol (Paul Aurelien) arrived from Wales. He had come via Cornwall, crossing first to the island of Ouessant (Ushant) and then making his way eastwards across what is now northern Finistère with a small group of followers. Here at their destination at last, they paused at Gourveau, near the port of Pempoul, where the saint struck a spring from the ground. It still flows into a huge *lavoir* or washing place, once used for bleaching locally made cloth. On this spot Saint Pol met a swineherd who agreed to take the incomers to his master Withur, a nobleman based on the Île de Batz. First they came to the deserted remains of a Roman *castrum* or camp, once the accommodation of a legion. The area name of Léon probably comes from the Latin *legio*. This site was later to develop into the town of Saint-Pol-de-Léon we see today. In the Rue des lavoirs, the Fontaine Lenn ar Gloar, also associated with Saint Pol's early claim to the land, never fails to flow.

Prosperous thanks to a port and the cathedral, Saint-Pol-de-Léon remained the seat of a bishopric right up until the French Revolution, and the very fine architecture of many buildings to be seen in the town centre reflects this religious prestige. The bishop's palace is now the Town Hall, and the fine Renaissance Maison prébendale in the Place de petit cloître has emblematic carvings of a lion and dragon, the latter being the icon of Saint Pol. However, when the new system of departments was established in 1790, the decision was for one bishop only in each new territory, and Quimper became the religious centre of Finistère. (The cathedral of Saint Pol would eventually be granted the status of a basilica in 1901.) This left Saint-Pol-de-Léon to a state of decline during the 19th century. In 1847 the great author Flaubert visited and called it a 'dead town'. But fortunes changed with the arrival of a railway connection in 1883, which facilitated the development of a vigorous economy based on the production of vegetables in the rich soil of Léon.

Today the town is a most attractive place to visit with many shops and restaurants around the historic centre dominated by the cathedral. At the other end of the main street is the Chapelle de Kreisker, which has the tallest spire in Brittany, saved from destruction by an order of Napoleon to retain it as a useful landmark for shipping. Inside there is a Tro Breiz altar of the Seven Saints with miniature statues of the founders of Christianity in western Brittany. The tower is sometimes open for climbing to admire fantastic views over the Channel.

CATHEDRAL

The Gothic cathedral, with strong Norman influences, was started c1230 with the west face, including two towers, their imposing spires, and the nave. The latter was constructed in distinctive (expensive) light-coloured Caen stone. The choir in local granite, plus transept, ambulatory and radiating chapels developed over the 14th-16th centuries after destruction by the English in 1375. Impressive interior deatails include the beautifully carved choir stalls (early 16th century) featuring human figures and animals, and refulgent stained-glass, not least a magnificent rose window. There is also a niche with skull-boxes from the 16th to 19th centuries. The cathedral underwent extensive restoration work between 2016 and 2021.

Saint Pol is celebrated in a lavish reliquary (containing his skull, arm bone and finger) topped by a statue of the saint with a dragon at his feet. Beside it is an ancient hand-bell (dated to the 9th century), sometimes claimed to be the very bell found in the stomach of a fish at the dining-table of Lord Withur, the saint's patron when he first arrived on this site. This was mentioned in the earliest *Vita* of Saint Pol written in 884. Pol had requested this bell from the King of Cornwall before leaving Great Britain but had been refused. Its miraculous appearance in Brittany was taken as a sign of the saint's exceptional status. Three stained glass windows (1920s) in the large chapel behind show the highlights of his arrival and settlement in Léon, including ridding the Île de Batz of the man-eating dragon at Withur's request.

Marie-Amice Picard was born in 1599. At an early age she dedicated herself to God, undertaking to suffer the pains of martyrs in her own body. The stigmata and wounds began to appear, along with visions and trances. On individual saints' days she felt the relevant agonies – being grilled on a fire, pierced by arrows, even crucifixion – and signs of these injuries appeared. Accused of witchcraft by some, she was defended by bishops and pronounced a true Christian in the ecstatic tradition. She died in 1652 and was laid to rest in the cathedral of St-Pol, where a burial slab can be seen. She became the subject of a popular cult, witnessed by a pretty *fontaine* in the field near her birthplace, on the Tro Breiz route.

Saint Pol and dragon on Île de Batz

Cathedral

Cathedral

Ancient bell

Stage 1
Saint-Pol-de-Léon to Tréguier
about 140 kms

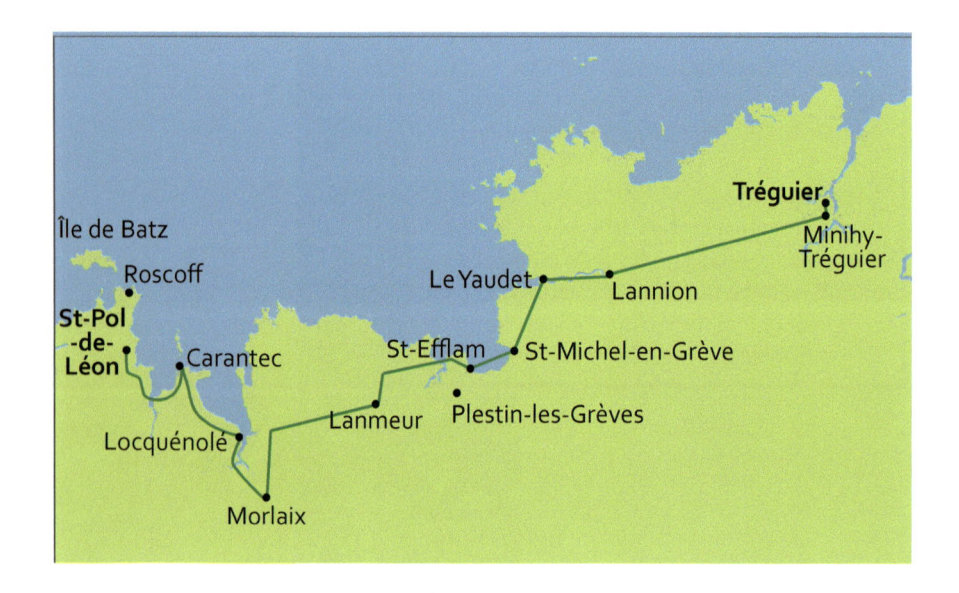

OVERVIEW

This varied stage offers much waterside walking, with coastal, estuary and river scenery, and some very quiet inland paths through farmland. From Saint-Pol-de-Léon, the Bay of Morlaix reveals its riches before the wooded banks of the Morlaix river lead all the way to the historic town itself. Lanmeur offers an introduction to the mysterious world of Breton legend that so often underpins reality in western Brittany and flavours this pilgrimage in particular. A wide perspective opens up at the immense Bay of Saint-Michel-en-Grève and then touches the historical gem of Le Yaudet, before a quiet reflective route along the Léguer estuary to Lannion. More river walking begins the final stretch across country through hamlets and the important village of Minihy-Tréguier to arrive in Tréguier at the cathedral.

Stage 1 ROUTE
From Saint-Pol-de-Léon to Morlaix

Château du Taureau

Very soon after leaving Saint-Pol-de-Léon along the GR34® coast path, the first example of hundreds of little chapels scattered throughout the Breton countryside is already apparent. The tiny edifice by a large dovecote is not in honour of a Breton saint, however, but Charles Borromée, a 16th century Italian prelate canonised after his death. A short diversion from the coast path further on leads to the Dolmen de Kerivin, a neolithic burial site which was presumably designed to be visible from the water. It was constructed in a T-shape with the burial chamber across the end of an entrance corridor, with an overall length of about 8.5m. It is a reminder of other forms of sacred space on this journey.

Small roads lead down to the Pont de la Corde over the wide Penzé river, and then the route continues towards Carantec, past two identical Resistance memorials to Jacques Gueguen and Ernest Sibiril who were instrumental in saving the lives of many British airmen in WWII by using small boats to take them across the Channel in daring nocturnal voyages. This coast has been the theatre of many conflicts over the centuries as well as a source of trade and profit.

The long strip of Île Callot, an island just over 2km long, is only accessible on foot or by car at low tide. A timetable is posted at the start of the connecting causeway. Apart from the natural beauty all around, the main point of interest is the chapel Notre-Dame de Callot with its low body and impressive heavy tower, on the highest ground. It has long been a place of pilgrimage, once attracting great crowds for the three Pardons each year, and displaying many ex-voto offerings for safety at sea. According to legend, the earliest place of worship on this spot was built in 513 by Riwal after calling on the aid of Our Lady the all-powerful (in Breton *Galloud*) to defeat Danish raiders. The name Callot is said to come from this epithet.

In Carantec, the Église Saint Carantec with its galleried bell-tower is a 19th century version of earlier churches here. It does contain an old statue of the saint holding young Saint Thénenan, his charge, by the hand. This mentorship derives from an earlier period of his life in Ireland, and he also has associations with Wales (Llangrannog) and Cornwall (Crantock). A curious King Arthur connection is mentioned in a manuscript in the British Museum. Carantec threw a stone altar he had been gifted from heaven into the sea, promising to evangelise wherever it landed. He arrived in Somerset to find King Arthur had taken it to use as a dining-table. The king promised to reveal its whereabouts only if Carantec killed a rampaging serpent. The saint captured and sent away this beast and Arthur had to return the altar, although he'd already been punished by the stone tilting so that everything fell off it!

The coast path here flows round the headlands just above the sea with great views over the Bay of Morlaix and the island **Château du Taureau**, an off-shore fortress named for the bull-shaped rock on

Causeway to Île Callot

which it stands (photo, p.41). The stronghold was built in 1544 to secure the mouth of the Morlaix river. It was brought up to date by military architect Vauban in the 17th century during tensions with England, and occupied by the Germans in WWII. Other uses have included a prison for sensitive incarcerations like political prisoners and feeble-minded members of aristocratic families, and later a more prosaic sailing school.

Unfortunately there is no riverside path down to the town of Morlaix and it is necessary to divert past an inland lighthouse to reach the attractive village of **Locquénolé**, or the sacred place of Saint Guénolé, one of the major Breton saints, with his fine church. This recently renovated building, with a galleried bell-tower (1681), has some striking examples of Romanesque carving on the transept columns. Nearby is one of the few surviving Trees of Liberation, planted at the time of the French Revolution, and on lower ground, the pretty *fontaine*, said to have been struck from the earth by the saint, is well-tended.

We then continue via wooded hills above the water, emerging by a religious landmark. **Notre-Dame de la Salette** is a neo-Gothic foundation, high on a steep hill above a former Franciscan monastery at river level. (The church is named for a village in the Alps where children had a vision of the Virgin Mary crying for men's sins.) It has been a constant site of Marian pilgrimage since inauguration in 1860. The stations of the cross continue on the wall beside the paved footpath which descends sharply to the waterside. In 1834 nuns from an Augustinian Hospitaller order took over the 15th century monastery site of Saint Francis to run a hospital and retirement home, the latter still in existence.

Finally the path comes out in **Morlaix**, once an important river port. It prospered especially from the cloth trade with England in the 16th and 17th centuries, shipping local quality fabric from the region of Léon. It has a vivid historic centre with stepped passageways (*venelles*) on the surrounding hills and half-timbered medieval houses. There is a large range of religious buildings, with two churches, Saint-Mélaine and Saint Mathieu, convents from the 17th century and the oldest of all, the Jacobins, originally a 13th century Dominican monastery, partly used as an art gallery/museum space today.

Morlaix was sacked by the English in 1522, when the garrison were away at a military display, although some of the raiders lingered to meet a brutal fate. A few remnants of the town walls can be seen, but the former château was destroyed after the Wars of Religion in the late 16th century, when the town supported the losing side of the Catholic Duc de Mercœur. The famous viaduct that dominates the town today was built in 1864 for the new Paris to Brest railway line, which brought much prosperity. During the Occupation of WWII, it became a target for British bombers, who managed to knock out one arch, which the Germans quickly repaired, but also to destroy the little school on the western end, killing 39 children and their teacher.

A unique form of architecture is one of the glories of the town. The *maisons à pondalez* were narrow town houses conceived for nobles turned cloth merchants who wanted to recreate their accustomed lifestyle in an urban context. Rooms to front and back on each floor branch off a turning stair. The name *pondalez* may possibly refer to going across these little 'bridges' to access the living spaces. On the ground floor are monumental château-style fireplaces, with the central space rising to the roof.

The Tro Breiz route crosses the river in Morlaix to move from the historic region of Léon into another, the Trégor. On the Quay de Trégiuer is the **Fontaine aux anglais** (1716 version), which is said to have run red with the blood of more than 600 slaughtered English who had got drunk on their spoils after the raid of 1522 and were caught by the returning garrison.

Saint Carantec

Locquénolé

Locquénolé

Morlaix, maison pondalez, N° 9 Grand Rue

Fontaine aux anglais, Morlaix

Stage 1 ROUTE
Morlaix to Saint-Efflam

After following the wooded estuary of the Dorduff, the way turns cross-country towards **Lanmeur** (in Breton 'the large monastery or hermitage'). The **Église Saint Mélar** is an important site in the world of Breton saints, reflecting Dark Age legends. The ancient crypt is said to be the burial place of this young man who was mutilated and then murdered by his usurping uncle, already the killer of Mélar's father. Rivod ordered that Mélar's right hand and left foot should be cut off, to prevent him wielding a sword or riding a horse. But a miracle saw a silver hand and bronze foot grow in place of the amputations.

Mélar was later sent away to what he thought was the house of friends, but he was decapitated there soon after. The tragic story is told in wooden panels on the pulpit. The pillars in the atmospheric crypt, with their strange decoration (plants or snakes), have attracted much attention, and there is also a mysterious water source that never fails. Legend says it will one day flood the whole area.

Nearby is the **chapel of Notre-Dame-de-Kernitron**, an important centre of Marian pilgrimage. The Gothic façade belies its much earlier origins. A monastery here is said to have been founded by Saint Samson, bishop of Dol-de-Bretagne, in the 6th century. Today the 12th century nave retains some Romanesque decoration in the carved capitals. Curiously a local claim says that it will be the only place of refuge from the flood...

The **Domaine de Kerveguen** is a cider farm near Guimaëc, based in a 16th century manor house. The Tro Breiz path leads through the grounds and walkers can visit the prominent dovecote in passing. Soon after, pilgrims will be happy to discover the **Chapelle Notre-Dame des Joies** after a short uphill climb. It offers a pleasant viewpoint for a break, and when open in the summer months, the interesting sight of a very unusual rood-screen in the simple interior. The quickest way down to the coast then passes the **Chapelle de Linguez**, built on the site of an early hermitage.

Soon after crossing the long bridge at Toul an Héry, the **Chapelle Sainte Barbe** with its ancient porch and stone pilgrims' donation box, can be found in an idyllic enclave of old houses beside the estuary. Saint Barbara was the patron saint of the coastguards once stationed here in the light of threat from England. Just off the narrow footpath that leads inland from the chapel is a beautifully secret verdant corner with the simple *fontaine*.

The route emerges on the splendid coast at the **Chapelle Saint Efflam**. The current chapel dates from an 1888 restoration, but it is said to be on the spot of Efflam's original hermitage. This 5th century Breton saint was by birth an Irish prince, but he ran away from his bride Enora on their wedding day to avoid breaking vows of chastity and devotion to God. He left Ireland and sailed to Brittany to settle in this area. Enora later followed him and set up her own simple hermitage a little distance away. Their mini-statues are displayed on the exterior of the chapel.

Saint Efflam had a strange encounter with King Arthur, who had failed to overcome a vicious dragon which lived on nearby Grand Rocher. He asked the saint to do the job, and Efflam achieved this by the simple expedient of holding up his cross in the face of the beast, which then hurled itself into the sea. This is not the only anti-heroic image of Arthur in the Breton tradition.

Stone steps lead down from the chapel to an elaborate *fontaine* and another stone money-box for donations. Many pilgrims passed this way over the centuries on the Tro Breiz or on the way to Mont St-Michel, perhaps as part of the Compostela trail. The sacred spring acquired a reputation for divinatory powers, such as indicating if a wife was unfaithful by casting three pieces of bread into the water. These represented the husband and wife and the saint. If the latter moved away from the couple, it confirmed the infidelity...

From the chapel of Saint Efflam it is possible to cross the sea-bed of this huge bay at low tide for a real pilgrim experience and a direct journey of 3.7km to the church of Saint-Michel-en-Grève. Otherwise a longer walk beside the coastal road or at the top of the beach will be necessary.

Cider orchard, Domaine de Kervéguen © D.Wright

Crypt, Église Saint-Mélar, Lanmeur © D.Wright

Cross in the bay

Chapelle Saint Efflam

Stage 1 ROUTE

Saint-Efflam to Tréguier

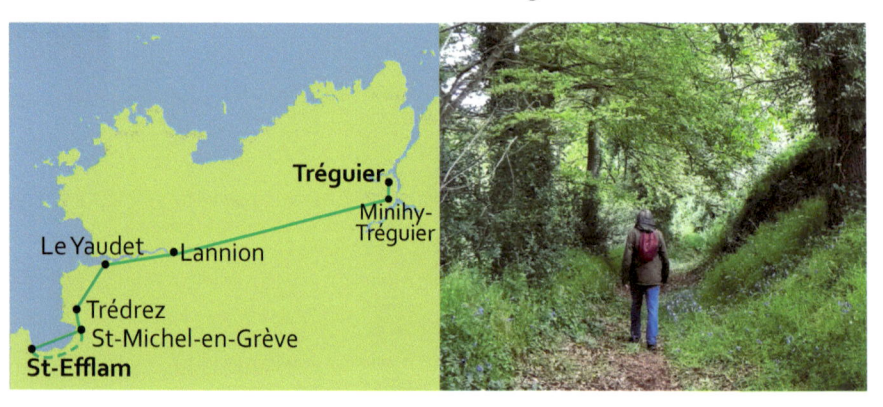

The vast **Baie de Saint-Michel-en-Grève** is dominated by the height of Grand Rocher, where robbers used to hide out to prey on hapless pilgrims crossing the sands. A cross (see photo p.49) to guide travellers stands far out in the bay, almost covered at high tide, to mark the half-way point of the journey to safety. This is a fairly recent replica, the ancient original having been destroyed during WWII. The shallow bay has suffered much in recent years from toxic algae, necessitating regular works of removal. In the village of St-Michel-en-Grève, the **church of Saint Michael** and its walled cemetery are directly adjacent to the beach.

We now take in two special settlements on the way to Lannion. Up a steep path onto the cliffs, **Trédrez** was the first parish of Saint Yves, who became the patron saint of Brittany. He was assigned here in the years 1284-1292 and is said to have prayed often on the cliffs and even slept there in the fields rather than in indoor comfort. The boulder called the 'pillow of Saint Yves' can be seen today by the church. This is not the building he would have known, but a later model with a fine 16th century bell-tower integrated into the western façade. Not to be missed is an expressive historical remnant of an **ancient paved way** linking the church and presbytery, where the saint himself must have passed many times.

Small roads and tracks lead overland to **Le Yaudet,** an exceptional site enjoying superb views over the mouth of the Léguer estuary, with a great variety of historical interest. It was an *éperon barré* or fortified spur in the Iron Age, and there is also evidence of Roman walls above the little port. Walking paths around the summit and slopes pass an impressive natural Hanging Rock and an ancient holy spring. The **Chapelle Notre-Dame du Yaudet** contains ex-voto offerings in the form of model ships, and houses a curiosity: the high altar representation of the Virgin Mary in an actual double bed, with the baby Jesus beside her and Joseph sitting in a chair at the end.

From here a pleasant walk beside the river via **Loguivy,** with a *fontaine* on the waterside and lovely church above, leads all the way into **Lannion**. After the destruction of Le Yaudet by the Vikings, this first crossing point of the Léguer developed into a major port in its own right. Wine, cider, salt, grain and wood all passed through the busy quays. Today it is a sizeable town and an important centre of the telecommunications industry. The separate hill-top site of the **Église de la Trinité** at **Brélévenez** overlooking the centre of the town certainly adds atmosphere to the pilgrimage route of the Tro Breiz, with 142 steps to climb to the precinct. Originally a 12th century foundation, this may have been established by the Knights Templar. The chevet and south porch from this period, both in pink granite, remain.

From there it is easy to visit the picturesque old centre and the **parish church of Saint-Jean-du-Baly,** which has stylised ermines, symbol of the independent duchy of Brittany, painted on some pillars. The Tro Breiz then takes the river route out of town towards Tréguier along the secluded banks of the Léguer. A little later we cross the rather battered remnant of a tiny **slab bridge** that may date back to Roman times. It is situated among idyllic tree-lined river meadows, a bright spot of Tro Breiz walking before the last leg to Tréguier, a long trek often on little roads skirting the Jaudy valley and town of La Roche Derrien.

Our next stop is at the peaceful village of **Minihy-Tréguier,** home of Saint Yves and the **church** he had built in the 13th century. This contains a fine triptych of the saint conventionally shown (in robe decorated with ermines) between a rich man and a poor man, and a massive text of his last will and testament on the north wall. Outside in the cemetery is a stone altar, symbolically called the Tomb of Saint Yves (whose actual tomb is in Tréguier cathedral). Pilgrims crouch down and scramble under this low ornate arch as a token of respect to the patron saint of Brittany, particularly on May 19th, the day of his Pardon.

From here it is only a short walk into the centre of Tréguier.

Le Yaudet

Saint Yves

Lannion, steps up to Église-de-la-Trinité

Minihy-Tréguier, the 'tomb' of Saint Yves

Slab bridge

Tréguier cathedral

TRÉGUIER

Tréguier was described in 1880 by an English writer, Henry Blackburn, as 'a place in which the artist and the antiquary would desire to stay'. The town sits on a promontory above the confluence of the Guindy and Jaudy rivers, with a port area below and the glorious cathedral dominating the upper ancient centre with its important ecclesiastical institutions. Here are many half-timbered houses, fine stone buildings and atmospheric alleyways, giving a sense of the medieval community. The late 16th century house where Ernest Renan (see below) was born is now open to the public as a museum.

According to legend, the founder of the settlement was Saint Tugdual (see p.27) who built a monastery here in the 6th century. Although the cathedral still bears his name, it has come to be associated rather with the historical figure of Saint Yves (d.1303), who was an ecclesiastical judge here in the late 13th century, and after his death became an official saint of the Catholic church following a papal enquiry. Evidence from witnesses was collected about miracles attested at his tomb and the good deeds that formed the basis of his reputation for supreme piety.

He was determined to bring everyone into the fold of the church and renowned for his positive discrimination in favour of the poor as a judge. All that he had was given away or sold to finance the refuge for the elderly and sick he set up in his own family house at Minihy-Tréguier, a village 2km from the cathedral. The chapel he had built there is still functioning and provides a second focus on the day of the Pardon (May 19th, the anniversary of his death), when his skull is brought in procession from the cathedral for a 'home visit'. This annual event continues to see the town packed with thousands of pilgrims, including lawyers from all over the world, as he is also their patron.

Outside the cathedral is the controversial statue of Ernest Renan (1823-1892) and the classical goddess of Reason, Athena. Renan was a native of Tréguier, who grew up with a religious background and was actually ordained a priest, but came, as an academic philosopher and historian, to write rationalist texts that offended many Catholics. His Life of Jesus, portraying a man rather than the Son of God, was highly controversial and regarded as blasphemous by the Church.

It was a provocative move in 1903 for the Progressive party, with the backing of the Republican government in Paris, to install these figures so close to the cathedral, an action bitterly resented by Catholic traditionalists. The day of the inauguration saw considerable unrest and tensions between the two groups. Down on the quay, a monumental calvary was put up the following year in retaliation, with statues of Saint Tugdual and Saint Yves (amongst others), as if defending their own.

This lower town was the commercial centre in days of economic prosperity, with merchants' houses lining the port area. Some have square towers to provide look-out points over the rivers. Wine and grain were both important cargoes for ships that plied the estuary to and from the Channel. The cloth trade also thrived here in the 19th century when the process of retting flax, or stripping the stems, was a local speciality. Nowadays pleasure boats have taken the place of working vessels.

Athena and Ernest Renan

Port area

CATHEDRAL

The earlier versions on this site have left only the Romanesque square Hastings Tower (probably named after a Viking chieftain), looming over the delicate cloister. The splendid Gothic replacement (13-15th centuries) is dominated by the unusually placed south porch bell-tower, and its slender spire added in the 18th century thanks to a financial gift from Louis XVI. It is the only cathedral precinct in Brittany retaining the elements of church, cloister, cemetery and bishop's palace. On entering the church via the south transept, a wooden statue group of Saint Yves flanked by a rich man and a poor man immediately sets the tone of reverence for this local luminary. The cathedral contains an ornate replica of Yves' tomb, after the original was destroyed at the time of the Revolution. A second door in the south face was added to give more direct access to this venerable site for the hordes of pilgrims. The reliquary containing his skull is also on display. The replacement tomb of Duke Jean V of Brittany in the Chapelle au Duc is rather lost in focus of attention on Saint Yves. Saint Tugdual's original chapel is now dedicated to Notre-Dame de Bonne Secours, although the founder is represented in a prominent position by a generic statue, in bishop's garb. He has to be content with a chilly Pardon on the last day of November.

Skull of Saint Yves

Stage 2
Tréguier to Saint-Brieuc
about 110 kms

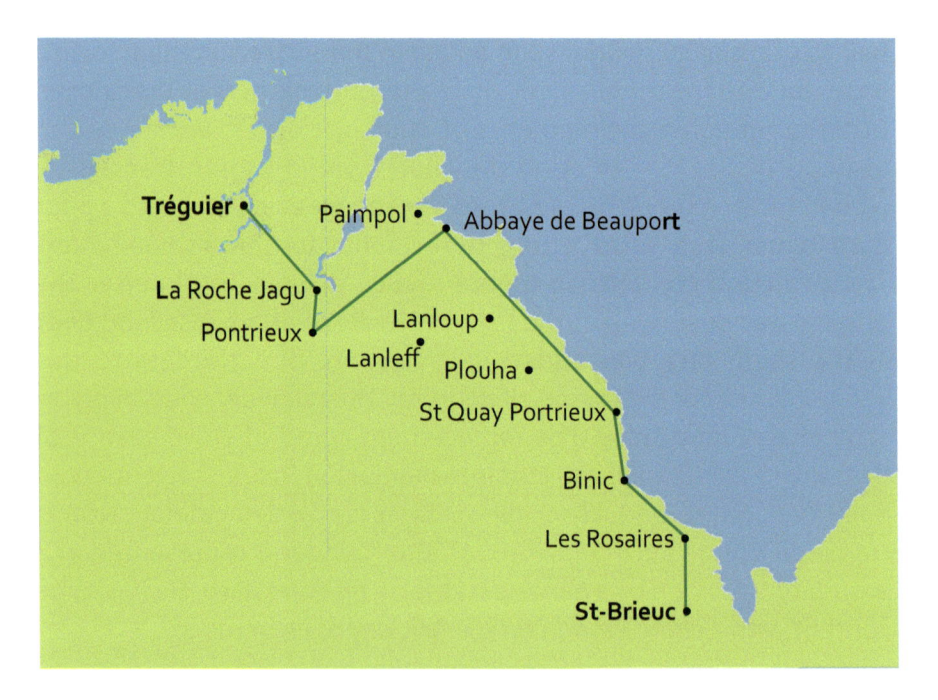

OVERVIEW

The first highlight on a route packed with interest is the landmark Château de La Roche Jagu. Then, after the flowery river town of Pontrieux, there are choices of route, with the option of forest walking by the beautiful Trieux estuary. Beyond the memorable Abbaye de Beauport, a long stretch on the coast path covers the cliffs of Plouha, highest in Brittany, so with some strenuous changes of level. Other intriguing places (such as Lanloup and the Temple of Lanleff) lie within striking distance of the path. The coastal route next includes the ports of Saint Quay Portrieux and pretty Binic, before an overland short-cut to the Legué estuary. A steep climb from the port leads to the centre of Saint Brieuc and the medieval cathedral.

Stage 2 ROUTE

Tréguier to the Abbaye de Beauport

Leaving Tréguier over the Pont Canada, the way then meanders through hamlets and the very pretty village of Pouldouran on a tributary of the Jaudy, towards the Château de la Roche Jagu.

The Tro Breiz route actually passes through the grounds of this unforgettable sight, perched on the edge of a precipitous drop to the Trieux estuary. The current version of the château was the result of rebuilding (from 1405) after destruction during the 14th century Wars of Succession (see p.71). It formed part of a defensive line from the north coast of Brittany to Pontrieux. The broadside exterior and unfurnished interior offer a detailed view of late medieval architecture. The castle is well-presented, and hosts cultural exhibitions. Its estate includes a medieval-style vegetable garden and an impressive horse-pond. Steep steps lead down to the waterfront.

Only three kilometres away is Pontrieux, where the Pont Saint Yves in this pretty town is the major crossing point for the Trieux. Little boats take visitors on the water to see numerous old washing-places lining the banks, today all decorated with beautiful displays of flowers and lit up at night. La Maison 'Tour Eiffel' is a famous 15th century blue and white half-timbered house, once a lookout over the river. The Trieux grows in stature from here all the way to the Channel. A good way to see its finest attributes is to walk through the Forêt de Penhoat-Lancerf on the right bank from Pontrieux, soon looking across to the dominant Roche-Jagu. The regular train from Pontrieux to Paimpol (20 minute journey) follows the same route for less strenuous and even more spectacular viewing!

Crossing the Trieux means leaving Trégor and entering the area of Goëlo, famous for the fishing ports of Paimpol, Saint-Quay Portrieux and Binic. There are very different alternatives from Pontrieux to reach Paimpol, or rather the special goal of the Abbaye de Beauport, south of the town. It is possible to walk through woods up the Trieux valley (as mentioned above) and then by roads to the coastal town, OR take cross-country footpaths to the village of Kerfot. The 17th century church here was badly damaged by fire in 1921, as a stained-glass window depicts, and restored soon after. The original is said to have been built on a crypt containing a healing spring and providing the entrance to a secret tunnel leading all the way to the Abbaye de Beauport, a route employed by Saint Yves to visit his friend the abbot there. There are certainly steps leading down rather promisingly into the earth beside the church, but the way is soon blocked. A more reliable itinerary to follow these days is a verdant path along the Corré valley which leads all the way to the abbey.

The Abbaye de Beauport is one of the most exceptional sites in Brittany, with the semi-ruined abbey around the cloister demonstrating a high standard of construction and decorative finish. Established at the behest of a Breton noble in the 13th century, it belongs to both sea and land, set in its own gardens on the shore of the sheltered bay beside the ancient port of Kerity. It housed a Premonstratensian community (canons rather than monks, devoted to pastoral work), something unique in Brittany. Remains of the vast Salle au Duc may indicate the need to provide welcoming facilities for the many pilgrims who arrived, especially those landing from England on the way to Compostela. The church was dedicated to Notre-Dame-du-Bon-Voyage, reflecting this important function. A modern stele with the figure 0 km marks the start of the long journey to Spain ahead.

Château de la Roche Jagu

Stele, Abbaye de Beauport

River Trieux, viewed from La Roche Jagu

Abbaye de Beauport

Abbaye de Beauport

Stage 2 ROUTE

Abbaye de Beauport to St-Brieuc

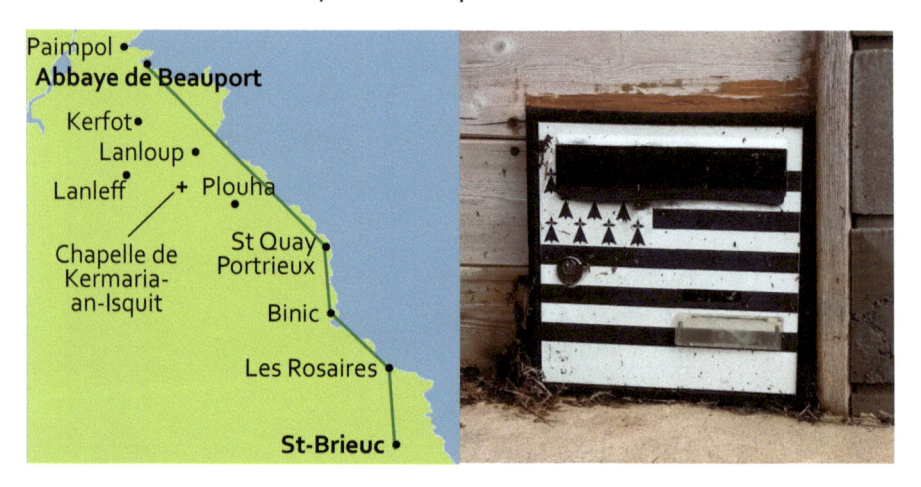

From the abbey, the easiest way to Saint Brieuc is simply to follow the coastal path (GR34®), with its sensational sea views and demanding cliff paths, also with the possibility of interesting diversions inland to see unusual religious sites. Moving south, the route soon passes through the territory of the Shelburne network, a resistance group during WWII, devoted to taking allied pilots, parachutists and French personnel out of the danger zone. These missions took place under the noses of German occupiers in guard-houses on the cliff-tops, as escapees made their way in silent files down the vertiginous paths to the shore before wading out to waiting boats. Plage Bonaparte was one of the main points of departure. Incredibly, no lives were lost and more than 150 got away to Britain.

There's a memorial on the spot where the Germans destroyed the 'house of Alphonse' which had been used as the last hiding place before making the crossing. Also, on the cliff-top nearby is a pink granite monument to all the escape networks in France.

The Cliffs of Plouha are a little over 100m above sea level, giving outstanding views over the Bay of Saint Brieuc. The coast path follows the roller-coaster contours, passing a rare sight at the little port of

Gwin Zegal where dozens of boats are moored to wooden stakes driven into the sands of the bay. These are actually tree-trunks planted with their roots and wedged by rocks at the base. It is an ancient practice, used here since 1854.

The Goëlo ports of Paimpol, Binic and Saint-Quay-Portrieux are emblematic of the area. The first two once sent ships to Iceland and Newfoundland for long-haul cod-fishing, a lucrative trade for the ship-owners who built handsome houses back home. Today Binic is a delightful seaside resort, with an interesting museum of popular crafts and local traditions. The displays paint a vivid picture of the maritime history that forged a unique identity. The name Saint-Quay Portrieux comes from Saint Ké, sometimes associated with the Arthurian knight Kay, who landed here in the Age of Saints and was attacked by local women washing their clothes on the shore. They

Off-route but worth the diversions are the richly decorated church at **Lanloup,** the curious structure at **Lanleff** and the 13th century **Chapelle de Kermaria-an-Isquit** with its famous Dance of Death frescoes.

The Temple of Lanleff is constructed of pink schist in the form of a double circle. Some see the shape as an echo of the Church of the Holy Sepulchre in Jerusalem. A Breton poet, Frédéric Le Guyader, saw it in the late 19th century as a repulsive, lugubrious place, where 'Death reigns'. The site is popularly associated with the Knights Templar (without direct evidence). Estimates of the foundation date range from the 10th to 12th centuries. Dozens of carvings decorate the capitals and bases of the columns with geometric, human and animal subjects.

took him for a demon. Left for dead, he was cured of his wounds by the miracle of a healing spring (now a *fontaine*) that sprang up nearby. The story indicates that not all saints were welcomed when they first arrived in Armorica. The town is known for its sea-bath spas and the fishing of scallops (*coquilles Saint-Jacques*), whose shells are the traditional symbol of the Compostela pilgrimage.

This coastal route eventually brings us to Les Rosaires, a seaside resort created in the early 20th century with a distinctive style of architecture, to take advantage of the wonderful 2km beach. Beyond the older manor house at the end of the promenade, a footpath passes uphill through woods and away from the sea. It then descends into a stream valley where a short diversion leads to the Chapelle d'Argantel (archangel), a delightful little chapel (15-17th centuries) which is open every day. After traversing a lengthy stretch of farmland, we reach a busy roundabout at Croix Lormel before continuing downhill to river level and the lively pleasure port on the Legué. From here, the most direct route crosses a swing bridge, and climbs steeply into the town of Saint Brieuc.

Cliff path

Coast path

Entrance to 'Plage Bonaparte'

St-Quay-Portrieux

Binic

SAINT-BRIEUC

The old centre of Saint Brieuc around the cathedral is perched on a hill high above the valleys and port areas of the rivers Gouët and the Gouëdic far below. Two viaducts take the N12 expressway across these divides. The town is the administrative capital of Côtes d'Armor. Its origins are said to date back to the arrival of Saint Brieuc in the late 5th century, with the spot where he first created an oratory now marked by a ***fontaine* with a magnificent porch** (1420) attached to a chapel, Notre-Dame-de-la-Fontaine, north-west of the cathedral.

The town does not show its medieval legacy quite as obviously as some others on the Tro Breiz route, as there is no château and only occasional glimpses of ancient walling. From the defensive architecture of the **cathedral**, however, it is clear that it could be a place of refuge, as happened at various times of conflict, like the Wars of Religion (see p.16). What most resonates in the central streets is the wide range of beautiful old houses, like the 15th century **Maison Le Ribeault** in the rue Fardel, with its corbelled frontage and artistic decoration, an indication of commercial prosperity. Many of these are now faded and unkempt, but their presence reflects the former mercantile success of the town.

There is an interesting **museum** (*Musée d'art et d'histoire*) presenting the two sides of the town's economic growth, with maritime and agricultural activities recorded. A further section offers stunning images capturing the essence of the region and its people. One old photograph shows the 1931 Art Deco station building (*gare*) which still exists today. The coming of the railway in 1863 (Paris-Brest line) greatly influenced the growth of Saint Brieuc.

The market square beside the cathedral has recently undergone a bit of a facelift, as the town attempts to create a more coherent and attractive central space. The web of narrow streets with one-way traffic can be quite tricky and intricate to negotiate, but the green spaces of the Parc des Promenades and the beautiful valley of the Gouëdic happily await the Tro Breiz pilgrim.

Fontaine and chapel

St-Brieuc house

Carved decoration on house front

Cathedral's stern exterior

Maison Le Ribeault

Tomb of bishop Guillaume Pinchon

CATHEDRAL

The building almost looks more like a castle than a religious building from the western facade, with arrow slits and machicolation more fitting for military purpose. At the time of the Revolution, the building was sacked by Republican soldiers and then used as stabling for horses. It was once surrounded by little shops built up against the walls, later demolished as a potential fire hazard.

After an initial phase of construction in the late 12th century, **bishop Guillaume Pinchon**, who held office 1220-1234, accelerated the works. Proposed for canonisation after his death, he became Brittany's first official saint in 1247. (This practice of declaring sainthood after investigation only began in Rome in 1234.) His **tomb** can be seen in the cathedral. In the early 18th century, the diocese sold a valuable tapestry (showing scenes from the life of Saint Brieuc) they had ordered less than a century before, to gain the funds for remodelling the nave, which was in danger of falling in. An ambulatory, used by pilgrims who came to revere the saints' relics, is lined by tombs and chapels.

The long period of achievement (13th to 18th centuries) accounts for the different levels of the cathedral. The interior is stolid, with plain round Romanesque-style pillars in the nave, but the eye is caught on entry by the modern huge ring of lights hanging above the altar in the high transept crossing. There is a fine example of late 18th century full-blown Baroque art in the **altarpiece of the Saint Sacrament** or **Eucharist** (although it is also called the Annunciation here), created by Yves Corlay. The stained-glass was mainly restored in the 19th century, with an exceptional window in the south transept on the same theme of the Eucharist.

Today the patron of the cathedral is Saint Étienne (Stephen), an early Christian martyr, although a **wooden statue of the founder Saint Brieuc** with two wolves at his feet stands in the choir. His relics were returned to the cathedral in 1210 after a period in exile to escape Viking raids in Brittany.

Stage 3
Saint-Brieuc to St-Malo
about 140 kms

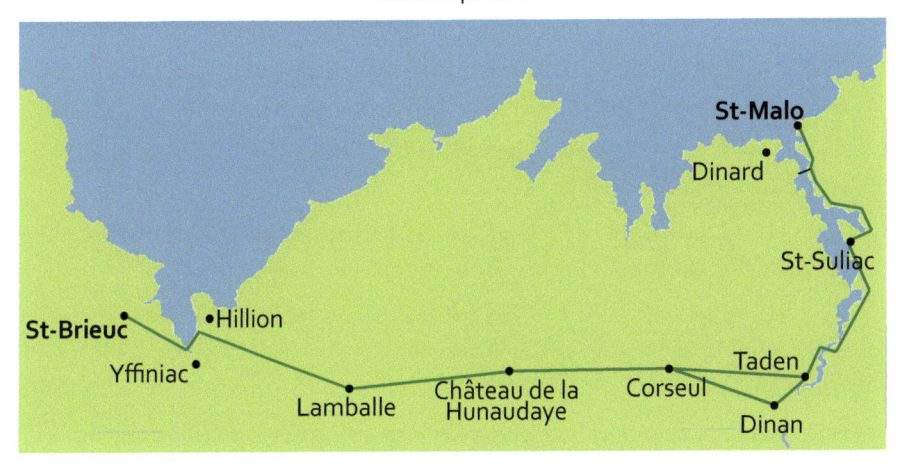

OVERVIEW

This fairly direct route starts in the memorable Bay of Saint Brieuc with its nature reserve before turning inland at Hillion towards Lamballe, an important historic centre. (An alternative would be a coastal detour.) From there the striking evidence of different periods of Brittany's history can be seen in the impressive Château de la Hunaudaye, extensive Roman remains at Corseul and the well-preserved medieval stronghold of Dinan. The estuary of the Rance then takes up the story via picturesque Saint Suliac to its mouth between Dinard and Saint Malo.

Stage 3 ROUTE
Saint-Brieuc to Lamballe

The route leaves the town via the deep valley of the Gouëdic and one soon has the sense of being in another world. On reaching the **Bay of Saint Brieuc**, the GR34® coast path provides stunning close and long views over this ever-changing expanse. It has the 5th longest tide recoil in the world, exposing vast areas of mudflats, sandy shore, salt meadows and dunes. Governed by the rhythm of the tides, these diverse habitats nourish a wide variety of flora and fauna. The depth of the Anse d'Yffiniac, round which the Tro Breiz route passes, provides a sheltered environment particularly popular with over-wintering birds like waders, gulls and geese. More than a hundred species can be seen during this season. The **Maison de la Baie** at Hillion offers a panorama and detailed information. The other beauty of walking here is the strong sense of liminality, passing through an environment that belongs to both sea and land.

From Hillion to Lamballe, the cross-country route involves small roads and farm tracks in unremarkable surroundings, although glimpses of the coast enliven the way at first. At **Les Ponts Neufs** it is definitely worth a quick detour to cross the curved viaduct built over the river Gouessant in 1913 to carry the Yffiniac to Matignon railway line. Now part of a walking/cycling route, it is 237m long and 27m high. After a lakeside stroll, more road walking leads to Coëtmieux, the village centred around the late 19th century **Église Saint-Jean Baptiste** with its galleried bell-tower. The nearer one gets to Lamballe after this, busier and noisier the roads. It is also necessary to cross over the N12 motorway and under the main Paris-Brest railway, then through an industrial estate – not the most attractive approach to the very attractive town of Lamballe!

Lamballe was the main centre of the powerful **Penthièvres**, a junior branch of the ducal family of Brittany. This status was accorded to Eudes in 1035 by his brother Duke Alain III. Their later ambitions for political supremacy were a major contributory factor in the tragically bloody Wars of Succession (1341-1365). When Jean III died without heir, the dukedom was claimed both by his brother Jean de Montfort and his niece Jeanne de Penthièvre, represented by her husband Charles de Blois. The English supported the Montfort cause, the French the Penthièvres. The great medieval warrior Bertrand du Guesclin (see Dinan) fought on the latter side. Ultimately, however, the Montforts were victorious at the Battle of Auray in 1364. But the Penthièvres were reluctant to accept a lesser position in the Breton hierarchy. Their château in Lamballe was dismantled in 1420 after an unsuccessful plot against Jean V which saw the duke seized and imprisoned, having accepted an invitation to a celebration. The Penthièvres lost all their lands and titles after this outrage.

Bay of Saint Brieuc

Lamballe retains many relics of its medieval heyday, including the blood-red half-timbered **Maison du Bourreau** (Hangman's House), a name resulting from the corruption of the original owner's family name Bourceau. The **Collégiale Notre-Dame-de-Grande Puissance** (Our Lady of Great Power), dominating the profile of the town from its high hill, was once the chapel of the château. It is a mixture of Romanesque origins, Flamboyant Gothic development and 19th century 'improvements'. Exquisite carving can be seen on the exterior columns of the superb west door. Nearby, the **Église Saint-Jean-Baptiste** was built in the 14th century when the Collégiale, becoming fortified, was no longer open to local worshippers. Despite much later remodelling after deterioration, it contains some earlier elements in statuary. The church also possesses a relic of Saint Teresa. The **National Haras** or stud-farm (once the home of royal stallions) in central Lamballe attracts many visitors, and the same location houses a very interesting **museum devoted to Mathurin Meheut**, the great Breton artist who was born in the town. His evocative portrayal of everyday life in Brittany, including many religious events like Pardons, is only one part of a formidable body of work.

> **Mathurin Meheut** (1882-1958) was an astonishingly versatile creative, working in various media to portray landscapes, seascapes and scenes from his travels, but most memorably of all, many aspects of everyday life, especially in Brittany. He was particularly interested in showing people at work, leaving a powerful record of traditional trades and practices, and in communal celebrations. In 1972 a museum dedicated to his genius was formed at the Maison du Bourreau in the centre of Lamballe, remaining there until the opening of a purpose-built structure in the precinct of the Haras in 2022. This was the result of an architectural competition, with the winning design by Françoise Mauffret. Here on display are more than 250 examples of Meheut's work, including drawings, paintings, ceramics and sculpture.

Viaduct, Les Ponts Neufs

La Collégiale, Lamballe

Stage 3 ROUTE
Lamballe to Dinan

This section of many forest tracks and roads of various sizes offers an impressive variety of historic remains, from neolithic monuments to Roman ruins and important medieval fortifications. The **Menhir de Guihalon** is a fine standing-stone in a wooded enclave, soon followed by the site of the **alignments of Saint André** in open farmland on the edge of the Forêt de Saint-Aubin, with a 23m passage grave. Both indicate cultural and probably religious practices from about 3000BCE. Such glimpses into the world of the New Stone Age again offer a wider perspective on what is sacred.

The Tro Breiz route next emerges from the trees with splendid surprise at the **Château de la Hunaudaye**. This picture-perfect ruined castle takes a rough pentagon in shape with its five towers, curtain walls, drawbridge and moat, with more than enough surviving to give an evocative notion of its prime purpose of security before comfort. It was built c1220 by the Tournemine family, probably charged with defending the borders of Penthièvre holdings against possible inroads by the nobles of the neighbouring Poudouvre territory, which stretched between the Arguenon and the Rance, and had a rival centre of power based in Dinan.

A quiet valley walk descends to the wide expanse of the Arguenon, passing a **feudal *motte*** from the 10th-11th century. It is possible to follow a demanding route (road detour available) along the banks of the river to the Barrage de Ville Hatte before passing through woods surrounding the (private) Château de Bois Bily. The simple **Chapelle Sainte-Eugénie** with its delicate window tracery is on the way to the noble ruins of the **Château de Montafilan**, perched on a very steep hill. The remains are partly accessible for walkers to admire the curtain wall with its ruined towers. Built in the 12th century by Roland de Dinan, it seems to have functioned only until the 16th when it was used as a quarry. The impressive natural site probably has a much longer pedigree. An inscription to the healer goddess Sirona (associated with the moon) was found on an altar stone here in one of the two chapels, indicating a settlement of the Coriosolites.

Their headquarters at **Corseul** was the centre of this Iron Age tribe before the Romans came. It is labelled Fanum Martis, Temple of Mars, on ancient maps. In Corseul itself there are extensive Roman remains, showing the foundations of a typical street of houses and shops, and a villa site nearby. Today the Eglise Saint-Pierre has a Roman *stele* in honour of Silicia Namgidde, dedicated by her son, Caius Flavius

Château de la Hunaudaye

Ianuarius. This touching vignette of life in the Roman Empire shows she had come from North Africa to be with him, and died in Corseul, aged 65. An excellent interpretation centre, **Coriosolis**, in a former school building, displays finds and evokes the heyday of this important town. The Tro Breiz route passes through the centre and then mounts to the large precinct of the **Temple of Mars** about 2km away. A Roman road ran from Corseul to Dol-de-Bretagne via Taden.

> **NOTE:** the unmissable historic town of **Dinan** can be visited now during Stage 3, on the way to Saint Malo, OR as part of the route of Stage 5, journeying from Dol-de-Bretagne to Vannes. It is possible to go from Corseul directly to Taden, by-passing Dinan for the moment. Pilgrims choosing the Taden option will have the chance to admire the late 14th century Grand'Cour, an imposing manor house in the centre of the village.

Dinan's impressive fortifications are especially apparent from river-level: it has the largest walled enclosure in Brittany, the ramparts now part of a walking circuit with exceptional views. The formidable **château**, built from 1380, offers well-presented perspectives of the town's eventful history. **Rue Jerzual**, a much-photographed cobbled street, leads up the arduous slope from the ancient bridge over the Rance to a town centre of exceptionally rich architectural detail, including a dazzling display of colourful half-timbered houses. The 15th century **Tour de l'Horloge** (clock-tower) in the thick of it all can be climbed for an aerial perspective of the town's layout.

Dinan is divided into two parishes, each with its own church. The **Église Saint-Malo,** in Flamboyant Gothic style, has some refulgent stained-glass windows (1920s) picturing historic scenes, including the crusader founder of an earlier version of the church outside the walls preparing to enter the religious life, and Duchess Anne de Bretagne's visit to the town as part of her 'Tro Breiz' in 1505. The **Basilica Saint-Sauveur** is also said to have been built by a returning crusader, Rivallon de Roux, in 1112, which perhaps accounts for the eastern touches, like camels featuring on some carved capitals in the earliest part. Outside, the former cemetery is now the **Jardin anglais** (English garden), with wonderful views over the Rance valley.

The heart of Bertrand du Guesclin, the most illustrious of medieval Breton warriors who was born in nearby Broons, is contained in a cenotaph in the church of Saint-Sauveur. In the large market square (Place du Champ and Place du Guesclin) he is honoured by an expressive **equestrian statue**, having fought a duel here in 1359 with the English knight Thomas of Canterbury over the question of the latter's dishonourable behaviour during a truce. The local hero won.

In 1899 a Hand-book to Brittany was published in the famous series of Bradshaw travel guides. It counts Dinan as one of the most attractive places of all to visit, and gives reassuring details of an English Protestant church, an English Club and an English book club, with the 'newest and best literature'. A few words are also devoted to the biography of hero Bertrand du Guesclin: 'in his early days he was remarkable not for his learning, but for extreme ugliness, great strength and a pugnacious disposition, all which qualities grew with his growth.'

Corseul, Temple of Mars

Château de Montafilan

Dinan, Église St-Malo

Dinan, the clock tower

Dinan, Rue Jerzual

Dinan, Bertrand du Guesclin

Stage 3 ROUTE

Dinan to Saint Malo via the Rance estuary

Whether continuing from Taden or Dinan, the route starts up the left bank of the Rance to the **Écluse du Châtelier**, where the river turns maritime on its journey to the Channel. Here are good examples of the apparatus of *pêche au carrelet*, fishermen's huts on stilts, with frames for lowering enormous square nets into the water (photo p.99). From here the glorious Rance broadens, sometimes to a vast extent, and wends its sinuous way towards Saint Malo. The changing views and moving light on the water are constant pleasures for walkers in any season of the year.

Either bank of the Rance can be followed, although some parts may be impassable at high tides and require inland detours, and initially there is plenty of up and down along the steep wooded sides, with rough steps here and there to help with the gradient. Crossing to the right bank at the curving **Pont St-Hubert** is recommended, so that the charming fishing village of Saint Suliac can be included. From there the coastal path continues all the way to the barrage at Saint Malo and beyond to access the famous walled city.

Mont Garot is a superb vantage point overlooking the Rance, and it was the site of Saint Suliac's first monastery. Below in the river bed is a large raised 'camp', fully visible at low tide, claimed by some as a former Viking settlement and by others as an old oyster-farm. On the slopes overlooking this today is a vineyard producing white and red wine, an old tradition in this area.

From the royal house of Powys in Wales, Suliac (or Suliau) arrived in the valley of the Rance in the 6th century to devote himself to the religious life. The nearby village bearing his name **Saint-Suliac** was the associated settlement, and it is one of the most beautiful in Brittany, with a tradition of draping fishing-nets over the stone façades of the old houses.

The **parish church** containing the tomb of the saint has a stained-glass window portraying the legend of Suliac and the donkeys. These animals waded across the river at low tide and ate the crops in the monastery's gardens, destroying any fences put up to stop them. Eventually Suliac took more drastic action and turned their heads backwards before fixing them to the spot of their crimes. When the owners arrived to retrieve their beasts, he relented and released the animals but widened the river to prevent a recurrence!

Another window (see opposite) illustrates the extraordinary pilgrimage procession of local sailors, walking barefoot and in undergarments (in winter) to honour a vow of thanks. The year 1910 saw great loss of Breton life in the far-away fishing fields of Newfoundland, but all the sailors from Saint-Suliac returned home safely, hence their determination to show their gratitude. The coastal route passes the **Oratoire de Grainfolet,** housing a statue of the Virgin Mary, on a vantage point over the estuary. It was built in 1894 in thanks for survival on the high seas, and became a focal point for women anxiously awaiting the return of their menfolk. A popular pilgrimage visits the oratory each year on August 15th.

On reaching the barrage, which enables the production of renewable electricity, and crossing the Rance, the world becomes a much busier place with rushing traffic and the heavily built-up conglomeration of a thriving port, Saint Malo, one of the homes of Brittany Ferries. The coastal path continues, skirting the Château de la Briantais, a 19th century house and English-style park on the site of a former structure belonging to a wealthy *armateur* (ship-owner) family. The wealth accrued by lucrative maritime trade was poured into many fine houses (called Malouinières) in the 17th and 18th

Church of Saint Suliac

View up the Rance from Mont Garot

St Suliac, drying fishing nets

La Tour Solidor

centuries, with more than a hundred still in evidence in the countryside around Saint Malo today.

This whole area, particularly the seaside resort of Dinard, was popular with English settlers during the 19th century. The Tro Breiz route now passes through Saint-Servan, where the British residents once raised their own funds to build a Protestant chapel (1875) in the Rue du chapitre. Local help was refused because of staunch Catholicism. There is also an English burial ground here in the old cemetery. After passing the magnificent **Tour Solidor**, a late fourteenth century defensive structure at the mouth of the Rance, the little peninsula of Aleth offers a glimpse of the original cathedral of Saint Peter.

When Saint Malo first arrived in this area from Wales, he stayed with the hermit Aaron on the island which today is Saint Malo (now joined to the mainland), before moving to Aleth to establish the earliest cathedral. In the late 9th century a deacon here, named Bili, wrote a Life (*Vita*) of the Welsh saint who would soon be incorporated into the pantheon of the seven founders of Breton cathedrals. Bili was also responsible for bringing the relics of Saint Malo, who died in Aquitaine, back to Aleth. In the 12th century, bishop Jean de Chatillon or Jean de la Grille moved the religious establishment to its current location inside the Intra-Muros of Saint Malo.

This unforgettable walled enclosure can be admired from the terrace of a WWII fort at Aleth, overlooking the ferry port. Arriving here from Portsmouth on Brittany Ferries would be to set foot immediately on the Tro Breiz pilgrimage!

SAINT-MALO

Malouins, as the inhabitants of **Saint-Malo** are called, have long held a reputation for their spirit of independence and exploration. At the time of the Wars of Religion (1588-1598) they proclaimed the town a Republic as they would not accept a Protestant king (Henri IV), and the defiant saying *'Ni français, ni breton, malouin suis'* (Neither French nor Breton, I'm a Malouin) came into parlance. The town has a rich maritime history, especially as a base for the notorious corsairs who had official royal permission to 'course' the enemy, which meant hunting down mainly English ships in the Channel and further afield. Rene Dougay-Trouin (1673-1736) even pulled off the remarkable feat of taking Rio de Janeiro! A century later Robert Surcouf terrorised the ships of the East Indian Company, amassing huge personal wealth. More than a century earlier (1534), Jacques Cartier set off from here on a trip that led to the discovery of Canada.

Grand Bé and Chateaubriand's grave

The little off-shore island of Grand Bé, reached by a causeway at low tide, has a hidden surprise. Facing out to sea is the simple grave of François-René de Chateaubriand (1768-1848), one of France's most illustrious literary figures, often called the Father of Romanticism, who was born here in Saint-Malo. Before his death, after a political and diplomatic career in Paris and abroad, he petitioned the town council for permission to rest in this isolated spot, forever lulled by the winds and waves of his childhood home. His most famous work, *Memoires de l'Outre Tombe* describes his affinity with this place as well as his formative years at the atmospheric Château de Combourg not far away.

Statues of these famous sons of Saint Malo can be seen on the unmissable rampart walk around the edge of the **Intra-Muros** or walled town, with magnificent views of three island forts and Grand Bé (see box). The former castle within the walls now houses the Town Hall and a museum of local history. It flies Saint Malo's own flag in pride of place, and this symbol is carried by many in the contemporary organised Tro Breiz pilgrimage (see p.15). One tower has the unusual name of Quic-en-Groigne (in spite of complaints), as it was built by Anne, duchess of Brittany, against the will of locals.

The historic centre inside the Intra-Muros firmly encloses the cathedral within a mesh of narrow streets of tall houses, with the spire popping into view here and there as an aid to orientation. This whole area was painstakingly restored detail by detail after the destruction during WWII in August 1944 by allied artillery and aerial attack against the German garrison. The 18th century façades on the quays, most effectively seen from Brittany Ferries boats arriving and leaving their base here, are a memorable sight.

CATHEDRAL

The patron is Saint Vincent of Saragossa, an early 4th century Spanish martyr of persecution by the Roman emperor Diocletian. A far cry from the semi-legendary Maclow or Malo who is said to have arrived on this spot from Wales and stayed with Aaron, the hermit already established on a rocky peak where his little chapel stands today just north of the cathedral. Malo then set up a monastery and became the first bishop at nearby Aleth (see p.28). In the cathedral transept Chapel of Peace there are statues of Saint Vincent and Saint Malo, side by side. The meeting of Aaron and Malo is depicted in a stained-glass window in the nave.

In 1145 bishop Jean Chatillon, or Jean de la Grille, moved the religious centre to what is now Saint Malo and built the cathedral in Romanesque style. Some remains of the original cloister can still be seen today outside, and the central nave and transept crossing in the interior of the cathedral retain ancient elements. Development continued through the centuries, with Gothic and Neoclassical elements predominating in the current form which is a true mixture of styles. The spire was added as late as 1860, and extensive renovation was needed after the damage inflicted by bombing in WWII. The stained glass dates from this post-war period, with a stunning rose window by Jean le Moal and another dedicated to the Tro Breiz in the nave, with Guillaume (see p.24) replacing Saint Brieuc in the line-up. The cathedral also contains the tombs of Rene Dougay-Trouin, Jacques Cartier and Bishop Jean de la Grille. The latter was given his epithet on account of a grill once being placed before his tomb because of the number of pilgrims visiting.

Detail of the Tro Breiz window

Saint Malo

St-Malo, Intra Muros

St-Malo castle

Cathedral

Rose window

Stage 4
Saint-Malo to Dol-de-Bretagne
about 45 kms

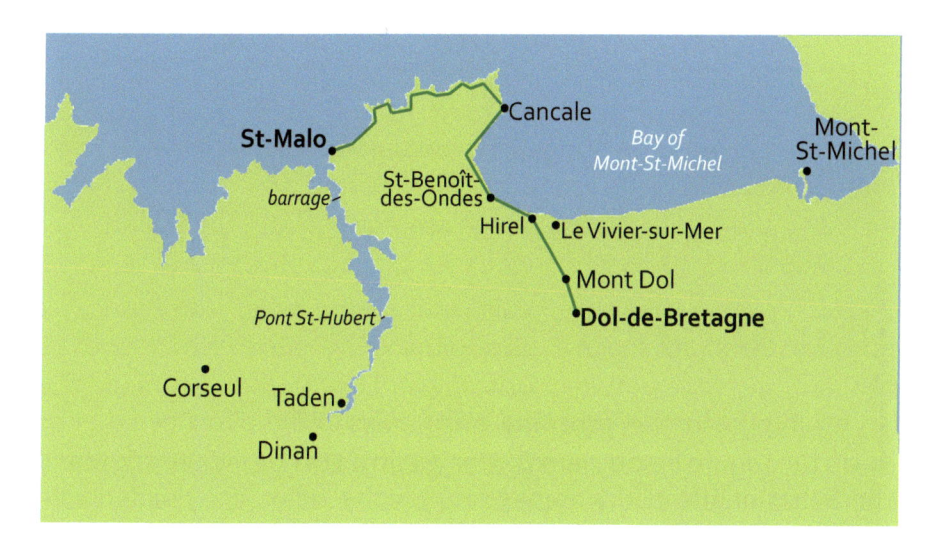

OVERVIEW

This is by far the shortest of the seven stages of the Tro Breiz, but the journey is nevertheless studded with historical, religious and cultural interest. It also affords distant glimpses of the iconic Mont St Michel, so long a focus for pilgrims in its own right. The historic towns of Saint Malo, renowned for its maritime prowess, and Dol-de-Bretagne, unique in the religious heritage of Brittany, frame a primarily coastal environment, with the added highlight of the otherworldly Mont Dol. The route begins along the ups and downs of the coast path via Cancale, before entering the immense expanse of the Bay of Mont-Saint-Michel. Here it turns inland across reclaimed lands to the striking slopes of Mont Dol before continuing into the town of Dol-de-Bretagne itself.

Stage 4 ROUTE
Saint-Malo to Cancale

Leaving the Intra-Muros, there are views of three fortified islands in the bay, before a superb open walk of several kilometres along the Sillon or the beach depending on the tides. This leads to Le Minihic and the Pointe de la Varde with its ruined fort before a curiosity awaiting at **Rothéneuf**. Here on the cliff-face in a superbly scenic setting, are the quirky sculptures created between 1895 and 1907 by a reclusive priest, Abbé Fouré. Many represent the families of local pirates, but there are also animals and sea-monsters, more than 300 figures in all. Soon after, a coast-guards' look-out on the headland has been converted into a **tiny chapel, Notre-Dame des Flots**, with ex-votives for lives saved at sea.

The coast here with its many promontories and islands makes for invigorating walking, with a constantly changing panorama. It may also be necessary in places to adapt at high tide with diversions onto firmer ground, especially around La Guimorais. In the Anse du Guesclin with its long sandy beach, beside the main road is a *calvaire* **and memorial statue to the Irish saint Columban**, who is said to have paused here in 580 before continuing his travels of evangelisation in Europe. The nearest village is named Saint-Coulomb. Visible just off-shore from the beach is the Fort du Guesclin, a private island.

In an elevated position above the Plage du Verger is the **Chapelle Notre-Dame du Verger**. This was created as a result of a vow by sailors who survived shipwreck, and also became a focal point for women waiting to welcome their menfolk home from the sea. The current chapel dates from 1869. Inside the west door is a huge painting of the Virgin appearing to the men as they laboured to remain afloat in a storm. The structure fell into ruin by the time of the Revolution, but was rebuilt twice in the 19th century and became a focus of pilgrimage for sailors making the terrifying journey to long-distance fishing fields.

After this short diversion to Notre-Dame du Verger there is the option of continuing by road directly into Cancale **OR** at least doubling the distance by returning to the coastal path GR34® around the promontory culminating in the Pointe du Grouin. This offers wonderful views over the Bay of Mont Saint Michel, and the Île de Landes just offshore, which is a nature reserve, home to thousands of seabirds.

Cancale is said to have been founded in about 545CE by Saint Méen, who is still patron of the parish church. A charming modern painting there shows him as a fresh-faced young monk in rough brown habit. He came to Brittany as a companion of Saint Samson, and later established his own monastery at what is now Saint-Méen-Le-Grand (see p.104). The imposing Neo-Gothic church also celebrates a more modern saint, Jeanne Jugan (1792-1879), a native of Cancale, who founded the *Petites Sœurs des Pauvres* (Little Sisters of the Poor), and was canonised in 2009.

The town is best known for its oysters, supplied to royal table of King François I in the mid-16th century, and a huge draw for tourists today in the outlets and restaurants lining the port area. A fountain near the church is decorated by sculpted figures of women wielding the traditional baskets as they wash the oysters. Historically Cancale also sent many men on the annual long-haul gruelling fishing expeditions to Newfoundland.

Rock sculptures at Rothéneuf

Cliff path

Chapelle Notre-Dame des Flots

Saint Columban

Cancale

Oysters

90

Stage 4 ROUTE
Cancale to Dol-de-Bretagne

The **Bay of Mont St Michel** stretches from Cancale to Granville in Normandy. It is famous not only for the eponymous island abbey of that name, but also the natural setting of a huge, shallow bay with tides receding up to 16km from the shore and then rushing in at high speed, taking the unwary by surprise. Quicksands are another hazard to be taken into account for safe passage. Walking out to the abbey at low tide must have provided a stimulating challenge for medieval pilgrims, a taste of biblical reference such as crossing the Red Sea. Much land on the shore side has been reclaimed over centuries for grazing and cultivation by a series of dykes and canals, with some parts under water at high tide to give salt meadows. The Digue de Saint Anne (beyond the Tro Breiz route), probably financed by the dukes of Brittany in the 11th century, was constructed to retain more useable areas. These *polders* provide a large flat expanse for exploitation before the land rises sharply. The liminal chapel of Saint Anne has been rebuilt several times after destruction caused by flooding and still attracts crowds for the annual Pardon on the last Sunday in July, with a procession along the dyke.

After a long, flat section of walking around the bay above the strand, through Saint-Benoît-des-Ondes and past several old windmills characteristic of this area, the route turns inland at Hirel and crosses reclaimed land on small roads lined by water channels. Then a very steep climb is required to reach the top of the rocky protuberance of **Mont Dol**, rising out of the levels like a massive cairn. This was once an island like Mont Saint Michel, before the reclamation of the *marais* (marshes) around Dol-de-Bretagne. To the north of Mont Dol these are of sand and sediment and called 'white marshes', whilst between the hill and Dol-de-Bretagne, the 'black marshes' are formed from peat. Quarrying work has left its mark in great gashes across the granite structure of the mound.

Evidence dates back to the Palaeolithic period with finds excavated in the quarry including mammoth, rhinoceros and lion bones, suggesting organised hunting traps. To the south of the summit, there are the remains of what may be the bases of neolithic dwellings. In the late 18th century fragments of two *taurobolia* or altars for bull sacrifice, perhaps part of the worship of the great Eastern goddess Cybele or the adopted Roman god Mithras in the Gallo-Roman period, were found on the mound. Historical imagination and the sense of sacred space is well-stimulated here.

Indeed, Mont Dol is a magical place with these levels of deep history. On the summit the dominant feature is a tower (1857) with fantastic views, topped by a statue of Notre-Dame-de-L'Espérance. Close by is a little chapel dedicated to Saint Michael, who fought the Devil for possession of the hill and then tricked him to get Mont Saint Michel in exchange. A rock on the vertiginous edge is said to bear the claw marks of Satan, and another, not so well known or easy to find, has the footprint of the archangel.

From the south side of the hill, which has a monumental cross (1891), the town of Dol looms high across the fields. From this vantage point, Satan is said to have seen Saint Samson constructing his new cathedral and hurled a massive stone in anger. This struck one tower of the building, which has never been reconstructed, and then flew off for several kilometres to land upright in a field. It is now known as the Menhir du Champ Dolent, one of the most famous megaliths in France (see p. 101).

In the village of Mont Dol below the summit is the **Église Saint-Pierre**, dating back in part to the 12th century, as can be seen in the nave from two ancient pillars with carved capitals marking what was once the limit of the choir. Above are faint frescoes from the 15th century depicting the Passion and Resurrection and, most famously, Hell, with the Devil and his helpers graphically torturing sinners suffering eternal damnation.

From the church the route descends to field level and winding single track roads heading towards the mighty bastion of **Dol-de-Bretagne** ahead. Tunnels lead walkers under the railway line and motorway before steps up into the ramparts. As a schoolboy in the town, the famous writer Chateaubriand walked this route to and from Mont Dol as part of class leisure activities in the 18th century.

Salt marsh

Reclaimed land

Mont Dol

Footprint of the Archangel, Mont Dol

Église de St-Pierre, Mont Dol

DOL-DE-BRETAGNE

Entering the town from Mont Dol on foot via the ramparts gives a sense of the stronghold position of Dol, rising sharply above the flat lands stretching back to the Bay of Saint Michel.

The town is busy and bustling, with a well-preserved centre around the cathedral, where many fine old houses were once the habitations of canons and other religious officials. It manages to combine modern and ancient in relative harmony, despite some gaudy advertising hoardings. Shops and restaurants on the ground floors of colourful half-timbered houses line the wide central street, which in part is called Grand'Rue des Stuarts, a reference to the origins of the Scottish royal house here. Walter FitzAlan, descended from a noble family in Dol, was the first High Steward of Scotland, and ancestor of the Stuart kings. The oldest house in Brittany, dating back to the 12th century, can also be found here, with a flower shop on the ground floor.

The importance of Dol

In the mid-9th century the Bretons became a united force for the first time to push back the Franks who were pressing at the eastern border, seeking to control the whole peninsula. Nominoë, a Breton nobleman, had been appointed by the Emperor of the Franks, Louis the Pious, to keep Brittany under stable control. But when Charles the Bald took over on his father's death, Nominoë rallied the Bretons and drove the Franks out. His move to consolidate Brittany politically was matched by religious ambition. There had long been rivalry between Dol, distinguished as a foundation of Saint Samson, and the archdiocese of Tours, whose metropolitan bishop had unwelcome authority over the Breton churches.

In 859, Nominoë created an archbishopric at Dol to oversee the Breton church hierarchy and give them independent authority, thus bypassing the status of Tours. The important lead that Dol assumed in religious authority at this time is shown in representations of Saint Samson (anachronistically) wearing the pallium, a white stole worn

Cathedral, Dol-de-Bretagne

only by the pope and metropolitan archbishops. This sets him apart from other Breton bishops in iconography.

The power struggle between Dol and Tours was to be long-running. Appeals were made to various popes by both sides over the subsequent centuries and the issue was not definitively settled until 1209 when Innocent III found in favour of Tours, and Dol reverted to a bishopric, one of nine Breton bishops, up until the French Revolution, when Rennes became the official departmental cathedral for Ille-et-Vilaine, to the disadvantage of Dol and Saint Malo.

CATHEDRAL

The sheer size of this Gothic structure is impressive. King John's soldiers destroyed the cathedral in 1203, and, through lack of funds, only one tower was completed in the subsequent restoration. The unfinished tower gives character to the imposing, yet plain, west face. In fact the traditional entrance was the highly ornate 14th century south porch. Much of the financing of the medieval cathedral came from the donations of pilgrims, arriving to honour the relics of Saint Samson.

Inside, the soaring height of the long narrow nave reinforces the notion of splendour, complemented by the oldest stained glass decoration (earliest dating to the 13th century) in Brittany. The founding saints appear in the main window, around Samson and the earliest bishops of Dol. The story of Samson includes a vignette of the saint arriving in Brittany in a boat structured like a little wooden turret (see p.23) The ambulatory is flanked by ten chapels, including the apsidal chapel dedicated to Saint Samson, with a modern sculpture of the saint on the altar.

The cathedral has many surprises. An unusual Renaissance-style tomb in the north transept for Bishop Thomas James who died in 1504, contains a portrayal of the Holy Grail. Curiously, this is lit up by the sun's rays on the summer solstice. Another notable feature is the double well, with one shaft outside and one in the choir chapel of the Crucifix, the two being connected by a deep underground chamber.

Tomb of Thomas James

Oldest house

Old house

Tro Breiz pilgrims leaving Dol

Stage 5
Dol-de-Bretagne to Vannes
about 235 kms

OVERVIEW

This very long section of the pilgrimage has many options for the actual route, and varied landscapes to enjoy. Churches, chapels and abbeys punctuate the entire journey. Important religious sites like Léhon and Saint-Méen-Le-Grand are included, but there is also the chance to walk through the beautiful Forêt de Paimpont, widely branded as Brocéliande, where the village of Tréhorenteuc has an 'Arthurian' themed church. Echoes of the distant past resonate in the form of megaliths, both standing-stones and burial sites, and later historical remains don't come much more impressive than the Château de Josselin. From there, an essentially rural route through some interesting villages finally passes the Landes de Lanvaux leading south to the outskirts of Vannes.

Fishing shack on stilts, the Rance

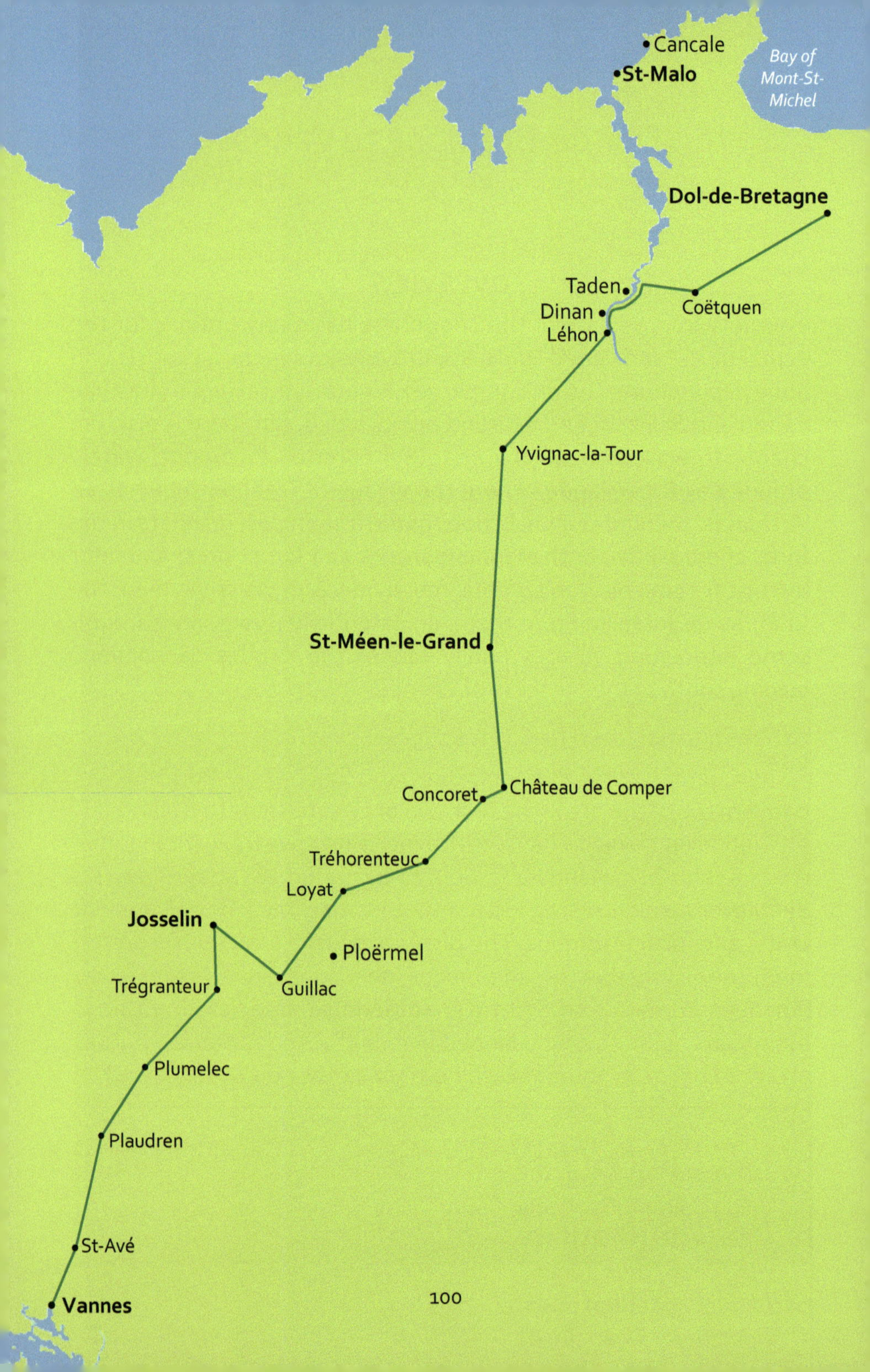
Cancale
St-Malo
Bay of Mont-St-Michel
Dol-de-Bretagne
Taden
Dinan
Léhon
Coëtquen
Yvignac-la-Tour
St-Méen-le-Grand
Château de Comper
Concoret
Tréhorenteuc
Loyat
Josselin
Ploërmel
Trégranteur
Guillac
Plumelec
Plaudren
St-Avé
Vannes

Stage 5 ROUTE
Dol-de-Bretagne to Saint-Méen-le-Grand

Just outside Dol, via the scenic valley of the Guyoult, is the ancient village of **Carfantin**, with an enchanting *fontaine* of Saint Samson on the spot where he first arrived in the vicinity and established a monastery. The name comes from the Breton *Ker-feunteun*, village of the sacred spring. The neo-Gothic church (1861) nearby has statues of Samson and Magloire (his successor as bishop of Dol) on the façade.

A short diversion from Carfantin leads up to the truly imposing **Menhir du Champ Dolent** (see back cover), a massive standing-stone (9m), one of the most famous megaliths in France. The very specific legend of Saint Samson and the Devil to explain its origin has already been mentioned (see p.92). Another, not unique to this stone, claims the stone pushed up from underground to prevent two brothers from killing each other in a battle. From Carfantin, the route continues through **Baguer-Morvan**, a place-name of Breton origin (in this Gallo-speaking area) sometimes translated as 'group of men from the sea', suggestive of the migrations from Great Britain in the Age of Saints. The rather solid church of Saint Peter and Saint Paul here was rebuilt in the mid 19th century.

We continue by road and track into the commune of Plerguer, passing close to the **Dominican monastery of Notre-Dame de Beaufort** with its lovely little chapel on the end of a range of handsome buildings in an idyllic wooded situation. The earliest fortified structure on the site was later replaced by an impressive manor house, with the current version dating to 1780. Four nuns arrived here in 1963 to start a new life in the rather dilapidated surroundings and today there is a thriving community. Pilgrims are always welcome in this place of profound peace.

Not far away is the **Abbaye de Tronchet**, another religious foundation in a verdant setting of lakes and woods. This was established as early as the 12th century, and although the handsome later replacement *logis* building is now a hotel, on higher ground the church of Notre-Dame de Tronchet and renovated cloister can be visited. From here it is not far to the **Forêt du Mesnil**, most beautiful of sylvan spaces, where the route passes close to an exceptional ancient burial site, the **allée couverte de Tressé**, sometimes called the Fairies' House. This passage grave, excavated in 1931 by the British nickel magnate Sir Robert Mond, is a remarkable survivor of the neolithic period. The tomb is 14m long and has carvings of (perhaps) goddess' breasts on two stones of the northern chamber.

Once past the express way, the route continues through pleasant wooded country to the lake at La Noë Davy and then **Coëtquen**, where there are remains of the **ancient château** of this famous family. Their coat-of-arms is the same as that of Lancelot du Lac, the Arthurian knight, whose origins are to be found in the Breton oral tradition. The little **Oratoire de Coëtquen** opposite has an inscription of the saying attributed to Saint Bernard: *there is more to be learnt from trees than books,* and another (in Breton) *Nothing and no-one will stop me staying the course*, heartening encouragement for pilgrims. The church at nearby **Saint Hélen** (dedicated to Ellen, an Irish monk who arrived in Brittany with Saint Samson) has fine 16th century burial slabs in the transept.

From here an uninspiring cross-country interlude leads back to the Rance at Le Châtelier (see p.79). The walking path on this side of the river is demanding in places, and goes up to the hamlet of Landeboulou before eventually descending again to the water for arrival beneath the walls of **Dinan** (see Stage 3). There is the option of visiting this dynamic town now if it was bypassed earlier, but otherwise the route continues up river to the lovely enclave of **Léhon**, with its old bridge, **abbey** and dominant **ruined castle**.

The Benedictine **Abbaye de Saint Magloire** dates back in part to the 12th century, witness the superb west door, and is full of architectural interest, from carvings in the church (the stoup, column capitals) to the evocative cloister. Recumbent effigies include various members of the illustrious Beaumanoir family. On the hill above the village, the striking remains of the castle are worth the climb, for the sense of a medieval stronghold and the views. A little oratory of Saint Joseph has been set up in the ruins.

The long route from Léhon to Yvignac-la-Tour initially crosses some attractive countryside of lakes, steams, woodland and a section of open plateau. On the way is the evocative half-ruined little Templar **Chapelle de Lannouée**, originally from the 12th century and later taken over by the Knights of Saint John. An **ancient pilgrim cross** is almost concealed in the hedge on the D62 crossroads 500m from the chapel.

Yvignac-la-Tour itself offers the **Église Saint-Malo**, which despite 19th century remodelling, retains some elements from its early origins. The restored west porch has impressive carved capitals with graphic designs featuring animals and humans, a decoration repeated inside in the nave. The distinctive 19th century octagonal bell-tower (*tour*) became part of the town name fairly recently, to avoid frequent confusion with Yffiniac, near Saint Brieuc! Just behind the church is an astonishing hollow yew tree, maybe 1000 years old.

From then a fair amount of road walking, relieved by several interludes of farm tracks, leads through hamlets, past the main railway line and the motorway (N12) before passing the little family memorial Croix du Champ Marzin. Next we cross the valley of the Rance, here a much smaller affair than the mighty estuary, at L'Équily. The route then rises straight to the **Chapelle de Benin**, dedicated to Saint Yves, but formerly, as a Knights Templar site, to John the Baptist. There is a very simple, pretty *fontaine* hidden 200m away.

The countryside context continues right up to **Saint-Méen-le-Grand and the Abbatiale** (abbey church), an important site on the Tro Breiz pilgrimage. At the junction of two Roman roads, it was a vital link in the chain of abbeys and religious routes. Saint Méen was a companion of Saint Samson, who also founded the church at Cancale (see p.89). His tomb is here in his eponymous town, as he died in 617 in the earliest monastery a few kilometres away, which was replaced in the 11th century. The relics of the saint, which had been taken away for safe-keeping during the Viking raids, were brought back to the Benedictine abbey in 1074.

A series of 14th century frescoes in the Chapelle Saint Vincent at the abbey, only discovered in 1985, tells the saint's story. He was known as a healer, particularly of skin diseases: hence prayers for relief from the '*mal de Saint Méen*', referring to a type of scabies. He undertook an early pilgrimage to Rome to pay respect to the tombs of the Apostles, performing many miracles and acts of healing during the journey.

Fontaine of Saint Samson, Carfantin

Abbaye N-D de Beaufort

Abbaye de Tronchet

Saint Méen

Abbaye de Léhon

Allée couverte de Tressé

Stage 5 ROUTE
Saint-Méen-le-Grand to Josselin

The route soon passes the (private) château and chapel of Les Gravelles, and the following trail is mostly based on the line of the old Roman road from Corseul to Rieux. Nearly 10km of hamlets, small roads and grassy farm tracks leads in a fairly direct line to the **Château de Comper**, gateway to the legendary world of King Arthur which the area now embraces. The original medieval castle was burnt down during the Revolution and very little survives. The current manor house, in its dramatic lakeside setting, dates from the 19th century. It houses the elaborate **Centre de l'Imaginaire arthurien** (Centre of Arthurian Imagination), with an exhibition space and activities devoted to all aspects of the legendary universe of Arthur and the Knights of the Round Table.

This is the beginning of a journey through the territory of so-called 'Brocéliande', as the **Forêt de Paimpont** has been strongly identified with this literary creation mentioned in the early tales of Arthur and his knights. (There are other convincing contenders, but the power of marketing has been wielded very skilfully here.) Soon after the publication in Paris of a popular book *La table ronde* in 1812, two local enthusiasts chose various locations in the Forêt de Paimpont to stand for places mentioned, such as The Valley of No Return and Merlin's tomb. This association is now the focus of the tourist industry and an important economic factor in this area. Regardless of branding, it is a most atmospheric and stimulating environment of exceptional beauty, full of natural magic, inspiring scenery and wonderful walking.

Three kilometres away from the Château de Comper is the bourg of **Concoret** with its distinctive red schist houses. The **Église Saint Laurent**, on the site of an older foundation, is said to have been built after a duel between two knights was ended by the appearance of Notre-Dame de Concorde. She reconciled the two opponents and they vowed to build a church in her honour. A stained-glass window in the church records this story, brightening the rather plain interior.

Near Concoret is the **Chêne à Guillotin**, an incredibly ancient oak tree (500-1000 years old) with a hollow centre. The story attached to this noble survival is relatively recent (1970s) and has developed from that connected to another oak in the vicinity no longer standing. The current tale is that a priest named Pierre Guillotin hid in here during the Revolution and was miraculously saved from his pursuers by the appearance of a spider's web which concealed the entrance. The tree is certainly more amazing than the surrounding hype, although it has suffered recent storm damage.

The route now passes up through the forest towards the hamlet of Folle Pensée (Mad Thoughts). From there, an optional detour leads to the atmospheric **Fontaine de Barenton**, scene of the duel between Yvain, the Lion Knight, and the defender of the spring. It is said that sprinkling water on a large flat stone at the head of the spring will summon up a storm, and this ritual has even been practised in modern times during periods of drought.

This area was the scene in the 12th century of the historical and extraordinary events surrounding the rogue monk known as Eon de l'Étoile, who went from a simple hermit to cult leader claiming to be the Son of God. His epithet 'of the Star' refers to the appearance of Halley's comet in 1145. His band of followers carried out violent raids on churches and castles, and it was said that demonic rituals were practised in the forest. Some see him rather as a kind of Druid, tied to nature not the religious establishment. Eon was eventually captured and tried as a heretic, but his clearly impaired mental capacities led to incarceration rather than execution.

A series of undulating tracks, with long views towards the end, leads on through the forest to the village of **Tréhorenteuc**, best known for its Arthurian themed church, often called the **Église du Graal** (Grail). This was the 1940s work of the rector Abbé Gillard, who presented both Christian and Celtic symbolism in the decoration. The Holy Grail, the Round Table and a massive mosaic of the White Stag all feature, and there is another striking example of this unusual fusion in the 9th station of the cross, where Jesus lies at the feet of the fairy Morgane, seminal character of Arthurian legend. The story of the patron Saint Onenne is also told in vibrant stained glass. A bronze statue of the priest outside the church was stolen recently, but plans for another in a less valuable material are underway.

Climbing to the rocky heights overlooking the lake known as the Fairies' Mirror, the route then descends steeply past the **Arbre d'Or** (Tree of Gold), an artistic work by François Davin symbolising regeneration after the terrible forest fires of 1990. We then turn off the major paths and follow a beautiful moorland way across the **Landes Rennaises** to a rocky outcrop topped by the **Cross of Saint Anne**, with wonderful views, before a short diversion to the **Abbaye de la Joie Notre-Dame**. This now houses a community of Cistercian

Cross of Sainte Anne, Landes Rennaises

nuns and offers hospitality to pilgrims and those seeking spiritual retreat.

Tracks continue across country to the valley of the Yvel, before the route skirts Loyat and reaches the long strip of the **Étang au Duc** (Duke's Lake) near Ploërmel (an historic town where the tombs of Jean II and Jean III, dukes of medieval Brittany, are placed in the fine church of Saint Armel). It is possible to pass on either side of this lovely lake, with a *voie verte* (Green Way) roughly skirting the eastern shore a little distance from the water, or a footpath along the opposite bank. If choosing the western option, it is worth a detour to **Quelneuc for the unusual little chapel**, of very early origin, with statues of Saint Mathurin and Saint Gildas. The tiny bell-tower was the only one in the locality to survive destruction at the Revolution.

From the far end of the lake, little roads lead to Le Vert Galant, where there is access to an old railway track offering secure walking to Guillac. Then it is only a short walk to the **Canal de Nantes à Brest** which runs right across central Brittany, here harnessing the wide, bucolic river Oust. We follow the tow path all the way to Josselin, arriving under the immensely impressive fortifications of the medieval castle. This was the late 14th century stronghold of Olivier de Clisson. (On the way, it is worth crossing the river on a very short detour to see the **Chapelle Saint-Gobrien** in Saint-Servant.)

Josselin is a good place for a stop-over as it has a **beautiful church and attractive streets of ancient houses in addition to the superb château** in its riverside setting. The **Basilica of Notre-Dame-du-Roncier** (12-15th centuries) is richly decorated and hosts a well-attended Pardon in early September. The legend relates how a peasant found a statue of the Virgin Mary in a bramble bush (*roncier*). He took it home but it returned to the same spot where the church was then built. The statue has been a focus of healing, especially of epilepsy. A connected curious story claims that washerwomen chased away Our Lady when she visited Josselin in the form of a beggar and so their descendants were cursed to bark like dogs. Various examples of this affliction are attested in the 19th century, with these poor women said to be cured by touching the statue.

Fontaine de Barenton

Tréhorenteuc, 'Église du Graal'

Église Saint Laurent, Concoret

Chapelle de Quelneuc

Tréhorenteuc, the Golden Tree

Château de Josselin

Stage 5 ROUTE
Josselin to Vannes

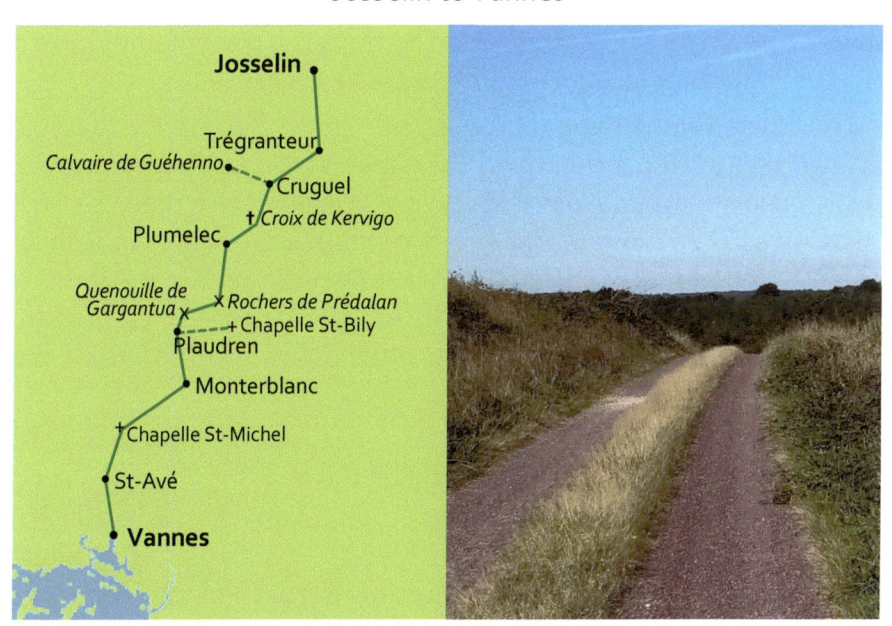

This part of the journey feels like an undemanding country walk with few major sites, but some great views later on. After crossing the river to leave Josselin, it is worth a look at the **Prieuré Sainte-Croix** perched above the town. The route south then passes through a river valley with its mills and up past the Château de Trégranteur (current version 1750) before reaching this most appealing village of varied architectural styles.

Unusually, the **Chapelle Saint-Mélec** in **Trégranteur** has a **column of justice** within its precinct, a reminder that cases were once heard in public in the open air. Melec's identity is uncertain: he may be a Welsh incomer from the Age of Saints or another of similar name (Mellitus) who was bishop of London and later Archbishop of Canterbury in 619, with a period of refuge from Saxon invaders in Armorica in between.

The way to **Cruguel** wanders through woods and over stream valleys with quiet road walking to join up the pieces. It is essentially farmed land. Many of the hamlets in this section have names with La Ville plus a determinant like a name (e.g. La Ville Geffray). This indicates a Gallo-Roman origin from Latin *villa* = a rural estate/farm in this context. In the central part of Brittany the place-names have a mixture of origins (see p.24), Breton, Gallo, French.

The **Église Saint-Brieuc** at Cruguel, with pretty flowered wide steps, is a 19th century replacement for the earlier version only a few metres away on lower ground, marked now by a calvary. Here there is also a heavily restored old *fontaine* with a modern statue of Saint Brieuc. (A diversion of five kilometres from Cruguel can take in the famous monumental **Calvaire de Guéhenno**, erected in 1550 in local granite, and hidden away to prevent total destruction at the time of the Revolution.)

On a quiet footpath we pass the ancient **Cross of Kervigo**, said to commemorate a battle waged in 938 by the local lord against Viking invaders. It is a small highlight in this unremarkable but pleasant rural ramble towards **Plumelec** (parish of Melec). This is a place that offers proud memorials to the past: just outside, a cross and 21 planted oak trees to commemorate collectively locals who died in WWI, whilst in the centre, the WWII monument is a huge menhir. On the way out of the village the route visits a moving resistance memorial, this time in honour of 77 parachutists of the French SAS who died on active service in Brittany. All these tributes to past bravery underline the sense of pilgrimage reinforcing important heritage.

We then continue through farmland and wooded terrain, passing the **Rochers de Prédalan**, perhaps a source for megalithic stones in the neolithic period, and the impressive standing-stone (6m high) known as the **Quenouille de Gargantua** (the distaff or spinning staff of his wife maybe!) to reach Plaudren. Here the church is dedicated to Saint Bily (Bili). This is the very same deacon of Alet who wrote a Life of Saint Malo (see p.82). He was later bishop of Vannes, and may have been the person martyred by Vikings near Plaudren in 915. (A diversion of 3km would take in the ornate cross, *fontaine* and chapel also of **Saint Bily** in more rural surroundings.)

Trégranteur, column of justice

Cross of Kervigo

Quenouille de Gargantua

Fontaine of Saint Bily

Chapelle Saint-Michel

N-D du Loc, St-Avé

113

The route goes on via the hamlet of Les Mortiers, as we pass through bucolic scenery, crossing the river Arz and finally reaching the commune of **Monterblanc**. Leaving there between the military camp and the aerodrome, the route climbs to the hill-top location of the impressive **Chapelle Saint Michel** (1524) with a two-storey sacristy added in 1831 to provide accommodation for the priest who came out to officiate from the town of Saint-Avé.

From here it is possible either to make a scenic detour via the **Camp de César** (once an Iron Age fortified height, with fine distant views of Vannes) or continue straight to Saint-Avé via the **Bois de Kerozer**, where the former château is a retirement home for priests, and an old windmill was converted in the 19th century into a reading room and viewpoint.

Saint Avé offers not only the parish church but nearby the 15th century Flamboyant Gothic **Chapelle Notre-Dame du Loc**, which sits at the junction of two Roman roads. It is also attested as an ancient Tro Breiz destination, where the relics of Saint Patern were sometimes on display. The interior is richly decorated, with a huge chancel cross, and contains an unusual statue of the Virgin Mary holding an open book to her infant son.

From there, tracks and inevitably, roads, lead into Vannes, the church of Saint Patern and the cathedral.

VANNES

The name comes from the Vénètes, the Celtic tribe defeated by Julius Caesar in 56BC before the establishment of a Roman settlement, Darioritum. The camp on the hill called Mené became a fortified medieval city, but the older habitations below developed outside the walls into what is today the Quarter of Saint Patern, where the founding saint's church (18th century version) still stands. It also contains his relics in a remarkable gilded reliquary, and has a Tro Breiz chapel with wooden statues of all seven founders. Saint Patern was probably bishop of the original cathedral, which is now dedicated to Saint Peter. This double association led to conflicts between the two as to which should benefit from pilgrim donations. The debate became heated and at one point in the 14th century, under threat, the priests of Saint Patern had to lock themselves in their church and ask for pilgrims to throw their offerings in through the windows! The most recent restoration in 2007-8 evokes the original 18th century baroque style.

The capital of Morbihan, Vannes is a beautiful city of gracious architecture on the edge of the Gulf of Morbihan. Impressive sections of the medieval town walls, towers and gates remain, along with narrow cobbled streets, especially around the cathedral, and numerous bright half-timbered houses of the 15th and 16th centuries. The carving '*Vannes et sa femme*' (Vannes and his wife) is a famous symbol of the city. An ancient market and court of justice building, La Cohue, opposite the cathedral, is now the Musée des Beaux Arts, and not far away is Château Gaillaird (1410) an extraordinary tall, thin building containing an exceptional archaeological collection.

Under Jean IV, Vannes was the capital of Brittany for a time in the 14th century: he extended the walls and built the famous Château d'Hermine, which was later destroyed (the current one of that name is from 1785). In 1485 Duke François II created the first Breton parliament here to establish a sovereign court independent of Paris, although it later moved to Rennes. The first step in the treaty of the decisive Union with France, bringing an end to Brittany's independence, was broached here in 1532. Much of the grand building of individual houses from the late 17th century was the result of Parliament being exiled from Rennes and taking refuge here in Vannes.

The rampart gardens below the walls are bounded by the river Marle with its old covered washing places, which leads down to the port. This was once an important stop for the wine trade as well as serving many smaller harbours along the southern coast of Brittany. It is now a pleasure port with wide promenades for strolling, perhaps down to the Gare maritime (1.8km) to take a boat to the islands of the Gulf of Morbihan.

CATHEDRAL

Vannes was already a bishopric in the 5th century CE, with the earliest versions of the cathedral destroyed in Viking raids. The essentially 15th century Gothic cathedral of today honours the renowned Spanish Dominican preacher and evangelist Vincent Ferrier (b.1350 in Valencia). After gaining a formidable reputation all over Europe, he was invited to Brittany by Duke Jean V in 1418 and spent a year of intense, exhausting work in the region, re-igniting the Catholic faith. Returning to Vannes in March 1419, he felt death was near and wanted to return home. He embarked on a ship to Spain, but it was driven back by a storm in the Gulf of Morbihan, and he died in the town a few days later. He was honoured in the cathedral in a beautiful round Renaissance chapel (1537), and the large ambulatory behind the main altar was made necessary by the hordes of pilgrims coming to honour this monk made saint in 1455. Recent excavations in the crypt have discovered the probable site of his original burial place.

There is also a chapel of Sainte Anne with a stained-glass window showing the pilgrimage of Sainte Anne d'Auray. Saint Patern shares a space and a stained-glass window (late 19th century) with Saint Meriadec (see p.120), at the entrance beside the oldest part of the cathedral, a Romanesque tower on the west façade. At 110m, Vannes has the longest cathedral in Brittany.

Vannes, the rampart gardens

Lavoirs

Church of Saint Patern

Cathedral

Saint Patern

Stage 6
Vannes to Quimper
about 210 kms

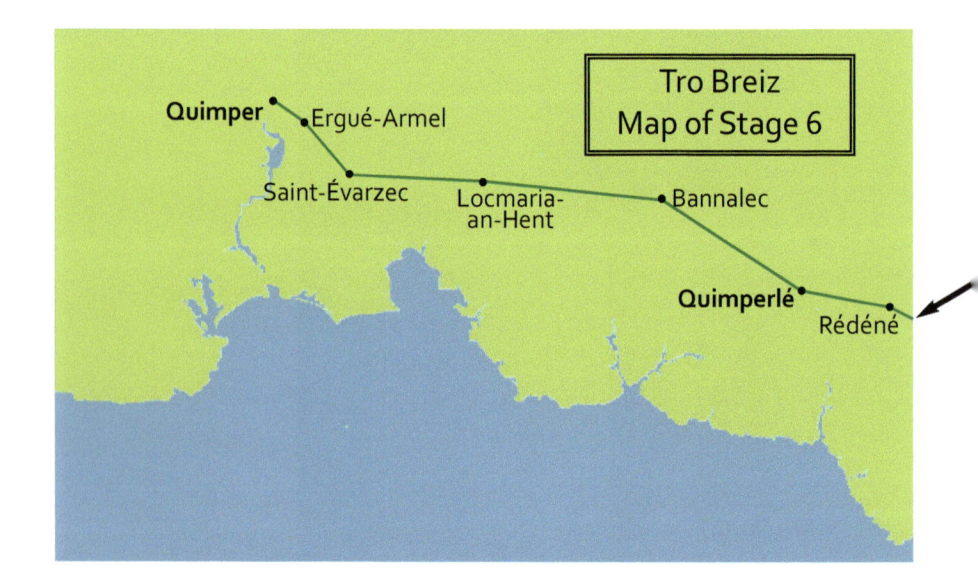

OVERVIEW

This is another long stage moving west from Morbihan into Finistère with very varied paths and some memorable sights, including the famous sanctuary of Sainte Anne d'Auray, the picturesque port of Auray, the extensive neolithic alignments of Erdeven and the Abbaye Sainte Croix at Quimperlé. The route is dictated in several places by the need to cross water courses via road bridges. Amiable Vannes itself deserves a proper visit at the beginning with much of historic, religious and other visual interest. The city's port also provides access to the Gulf of Morbihan and its many islands.

Tro Breiz
Map of Stage 6

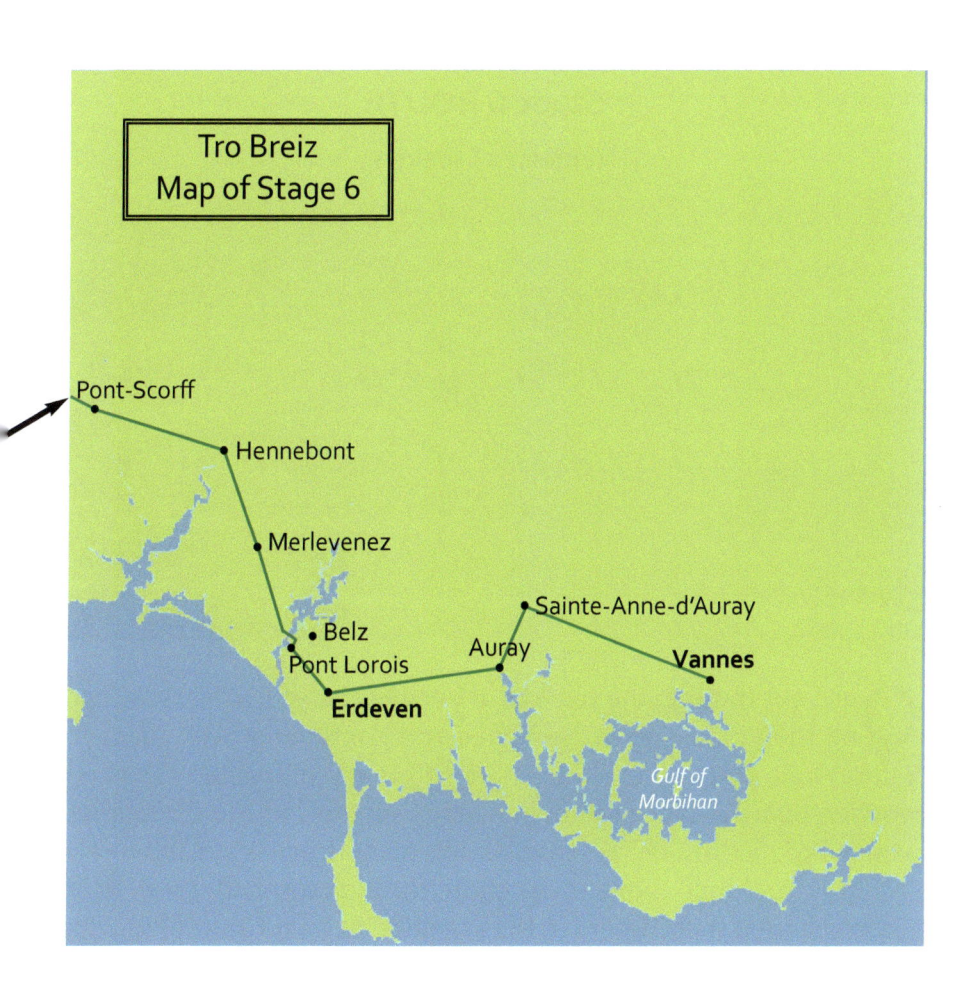

Pont-Scorff
Hennebont
Merlevenez
Belz
Pont Lorois
Erdeven
Sainte-Anne-d'Auray
Auray
Vannes
Gulf of Morbihan

Gulf of Morbihan

Stage 6 ROUTE
Vannes to Erdeven

Once out through the suburbs of Vannes, a useful Green Way can be found starting at Tréhuinec and continuing over 20km to Sainte Anne d'Auray. The track is a mixture of compacted sand and wooden boardwalks raised over marshy sections of the sometimes wooded route through farmland. Unlike most Green Ways, it is rarely straight for long! Signage is good throughout and there is a recommended short detour to the **Chapelle de Lézurgan** at Plescop. This was built in the 15th century by a former bishop of Vannes who had a residence nearby, and has fine sculpted beams. In the precinct is a huge neolithic standing-stone bearing a plaque with details of the building's foundation.

The Green Way also passes though the village of **Mériadec**, where the **Église Saint-Mériadec** was rebuilt in the 20th century on the site of an earlier foundation. Mériadec was bishop of Vannes in the 7th or 8th century, but some place him much later. Although said to be a native of Armorica, he has connections in Cornwall (as Saint Meriasek in Camborne) and Wales.

This winding, peaceful route leads all the way into **Sainte Anne d'Auray**, the most important of Catholic sanctuaries in Brittany and a major centre of pilgrimage. It is dedicated to the female patron of Brittany, Saint Anne, mother of Mary, who is said in legend to have been born in the region, or visited Breton shores. On this site in 1623 a peasant called Yvon Nicolazic first had a vision of Saint Anne telling him that an ancient chapel in her honour here had disappeared and should be rebuilt. Further visions continued until 1625 when Nicolazic dug up an ancient statue of the saint. The local priest, who had dismissed earlier claims, was finally persuaded to take the peasant seriously. In 1628 the first chapel was built with the blessing of the bishop of Vannes. It soon became a place of pilgrimage to honour the miracle of Anne's appearance.

The famous statue was burnt at the time of the Revolution, but a fragment remains in the base of the later version of Saint Anne in her chapel within the basilica here. This was completed in 1874 on the site of the earlier building which proved too small to accommodate the demands of pilgrims. The *fontaine* and monumental statue outside are on the spot of the first vision Nicolazic experienced. The founder also has his own chapel in the main church and a statue in the grounds.

This great complex also includes the **Scala Santa**, a ceremonial staircase constructed near the chapel by the local Carmelite order in 1662, where pilgrims would climb the steps on their knees. In 1870 it was moved further away to the spot it now occupies. There is also a very moving monumental **war memorial** (1932) conceived for the victims of WW1 and later incorporating other conflicts.

The Pardon of Saint Anne each year in July attracts huge crowds. At the end of the 20th century, after the visit of Pope John Paul II in 1996, the shrine welcomed as many as 800,000 pilgrims a year.

Primarily road walking leads to nearby **Auray**, and an atmospheric stepped descent to the river past the **Église Saint-Sauveur** and **Chapelle Notre-Dame-de-Lourdes**. The very pretty harbour of **Saint Goustan**, with its ancient arched bridge, has a plaque commemorating the fact that Benjamin Franklin was forced to land here on his way to Nantes, seeking French support for American independence in 1776.

The route crosses the river and follows the right bank past remnants of Auray's medieval fortifications before continuing through the high town. We eventually descend on a former Roman road to the little **Chapelle Saint-Cado**, with a carved cat on the gable recalling the legend of the saint who made a pact with the Devil. This was to build a bridge in one night (at Saint-Cado on the Ria d'Étel ahead on this journey). When Satan demanded his payment of the first soul to cross the new construction, Cado tricked him by sending a cat over.

Beyond the chapel a wooded footpath leads to the **mausoleum of Georges Cadoudal**. This significant leader of the Chouans (royalist Catholic counter-revolutionaries) operated in this area over a ten year period after the Revolution. Revered by his men, he was renowned for his bravery and strategic intelligence. When in Paris in 1804 to help organise a plot against Napoleon, he was betrayed and sent to the guillotine. The manor house opposite the memorial was the Cadoudal family home.

Some cross-country walking leads to another **Chapelle Saint Cado**, a beautifully simple sacred spot with a pretty *fontaine* tightly situated amongst old houses, offering a haven of peace. Soon after, near the golf course named after him, is the **Chapelle Saint Laurent**, with a distinctive *fleur de lys* design in one window tracery.

Wooded terrain then continues towards **Erdeven**, where it is well worth a diversion to visit the **Géants de Kerzerho**, stones of astonishing size, just a small part of the extensive neolithic remains here. Rows of menhirs or standing-stones can be seen by one of the main roads through the village, and down in the valley are further alignments including a stone known as Caesar's Chair. (The Romans had a notable naval victory over the Vénètes tribe off this south coast in 56BCE.)

A short distance ahead is the rather plain **Chapelle des Sept Saints**, obviously a Tro Breiz highlight, and open from May to September. Here the seven founding saints are honoured in statuary around the simple white-washed interior walls and in the stained-glass. The chapel was reconstructed in 1899 and renewed again in recent times. There's a *fontaine* of the same date 200m away.

Chapelle de Lézurgan

Ste Anne d'Auray, Basilica

Ste Anne d'Auray, Scala Santa

St-Goustan, Auray

Chapelle St-Cado, Ploemel

Géants de Kerzerho

Mausoleum of Cadoudal

Stage 6 ROUTE
Erdeven to Quimperlé

From the Chapelle des Sept Saints we soon reach a scenic path along Le Sac'h river, which leads round the coast, with great views, to **Port Niscop** (which comes from the Breton *En* Eskop, meaning a bishop) in a stunning location on the Ria d'Étel. Here beside the road bridge of Pont Lorois is an **oratory of Notre-Dame de Lourdes**, with many votive plaques, built by local sailors in 1952 to commemorate those lost at sea.

(Before crossing the bridge, it is possible to make a diversion of 3 km north to the picturesque island of Saint Cado, with its chapel including the 'bed' of the saint and sacred spring on the tidal beach. And, of course, the Devil's bridge (see p.122)!

After a short spell on the coastal path, we pass **Mané Véchen** the huge and elaborate site of a Gallo-Roman villa, probably once a centre of maritime trade between Brittany and Rome. Moving inland the route comes to the ***fontaine*** and **chapel of Saint Cornely,** an important figure in southern Brittany, patron of horned beasts. Many brought animals of this type to be blessed at the annual Pardon. Cornely is most famously associated with the legend of Carnac, where the world-renowned lines of standing-stones were said to be petrified Roman soldiers who were chasing him.

The route now skirts Plouhinec and continues across country to Merlevenez and the unmissable **parish church of Notre-Dame-de-la-Joie**. This essentially 12th century foundation with a later nave was authentically restored after suffering bomb damage in WWII, when the tower was used as a look-out by the Germans, who had a well-defended base in nearby Lorient. The interior retains superb carved capitals of very varied design.

There are now various ways of getting to **Hennebont**, but the most scenic route crosses the Blavet river at the Pont du Bonhomme, where the supports of an older bridge remain alongside the new version. The coastal path continues up-stream, before we finally turn inland and reach the outskirts of this historic town, crossing the river and approaching **the ramparts**. The name is from Breton *hen pont*, the old bridge, and it appears for the first time in 1029 in the *Cartulaire* (document of property ownership and donations) of the Abbaye de Sainte-Croix at Quimperlé. At its height this was an important port and gave the dukes of Brittany control over the passage along the **Blavet**, a major waterway to the interior. Walking along the top of the ramparts today gives a good sense of this strategic position. The formidable gate, **Porte de Bro Erec'h** is an indication of the strength of the local defences.

The town was the scene of a famous incident in 1342 during the Wars of Succession (see p.71). Besieged by Charles de Blois, it held out thanks to the bravery of Jeanne de Flandre, the wife of opposing leader Jean de Montfort who had been captured. She rallied the troops here in her husband's absence and for her ardour in adversity earned the epithet Jeanne la Flamme. (In the church, one stained-glass window imagines her holding up her little son, the future Duke Jean IV, to inspire the troops, photo p.129.) The town was finally relieved by the arrival of an English fleet, which sailed up the Blavet.

The 16th century church **Notre-Dame-de-Paradis**, now a basilica, with its narrow west front on the square, is a refined example of the Flamboyant Gothic style. The concept originated after the visit of

Anne de Bretagne on her 'Tro Breiz' (see p.31), when she said prayers in a little oratory on the 'hill of paradise'. A pious blacksmith decided to build a church worthy of 'Madame Marie' on the spot, although he died before it was finished in the 1530s.

A silver-plated bronze statue of Our Lady now replaces the original silver one which was melted down in the Revolution. The latter had been donated following a vow during a terrible outbreak of plague in 1699. An annual festival in her honour to carry the statue in procession was also promised, and continues to this day at the end of each September.

The route west leaves Hennebont past the **Église Saint Caradec** and continues mostly on footpaths and tracks across country towards Pont Scorff (about 15km away), passing the **chapel of Notre-Dame de Bonne-Nouvelle** (technically in Cléguer) at Le Bas Pont Scorff. A part white-washed chapel, 13th century in origin, but refashioned in the 18/19th centuries, this contains a curiosity. A recumbent effigy of a woman, in limestone on a granite base, measures 2,20m. (It may have been intended to be an external vertical decoration.) Her identity is unknown, possibly Marie de Limoges who married Arthur, future duke of Brittany in 1275, and in popular tradition the figure is called Notre-Dame de Tronchâteau (the local seigneury).

Next we cross the Scorff on the old **Pont Saint-Jean** (or Pont Romain / Roman bridge), a beautiful spot with the ruins of an old hospital chapel on the bank, and enter the attractive *'petite cité de caractère'* **Pont Scorff**, famous today for its artisans' 'village' La Cour des Métiers d'Art. Steps lead up past a modern wood sculpture of seven prophets by Pierre de Grauw to the square of the **Eglise du Sacré-Coëur**, built in the late 19th century, which lacks a bell-tower due to insufficient funding. The strange wooden structure at the rear served the purpose. The church stands near **La Maison des Princes**, a handsome early 16th century edifice in Renaissance style, now housing the town hall.

Leaving past the **Chapelle Saint-Aubin** at Lesbin, with two beautiful yew trees in the precinct, an undemanding 8km cross-country walk leads to the little *bourg* of **Rédéné**, which is just inside the department of Finistère. Here the parish church of **Saint-Pierre-et-Notre-Dame-de-Lorette** retains its ossuary (bone house), unusually converted into a side-chapel, with the mysterious carvings of two faces on the exterior. The route continues through the valley of the Scave and across country to the isolated **Fontaine Saint Adrien** in deeply wooded terrain.

Afterwards a combination of footpath and road walking leads to the banks of the Ellé and entry into the ancient town of **Quimperlé**, situated on the confluence of two rivers. Beside the bridge is the **statue of Théodore Hersart de la Villemarqué**, who was born here in 1815. He collected testimony for his seminal work of the oral tradition of Brittany, the *Barzaz Breiz*, and this collection of popular songs and moving legendary narratives offers key insights into Breton culture beyond their considerable entertainment value.

Across the river, the Romanesque **Abbaye Saint-Croix** (11th century) lies up ahead. It has an unusual central rotunda, based on the Saint-Sepulchre in Jerusalem. The building had to be restored after a bell-tower added in the 17th century fell in 1862 and destroyed much of the church except the choir and crypt below. In the latter, which retains its original columns and capitals, is the **tomb of Saint Gurloës** (or Urlou), the first abbot. It has a hole for pilgrims to place their head to cure migraines, and a larger opening for other body parts, as his healing powers also extended to gout and rheumatism.

In line with the Benedictine ethos, the abbey once had an extensive library, including many precious manuscripts, but it was destroyed at the time of the Revolution. Fortunately, a local doctor saved the *Cartulaire*, which provides detailed information of Saint-Croix's medieval property holdings, privileges and received donations. The original is now in the British Library.

Across the river Isole, a steep street leads to **Église Notre-Dame de l'Assumption**, which dominates the High Town of Quimperlé. The route then passes the old **Hôpital Frémeur**, of medieval origin and incorporating a chapel, with a figure on the gable end kitted out like a pilgrim.

Barzaz Breiz

'May God give victory to the Breton
and good news to all those in his country!'

(Reference to Morvan, who valiantly fought the Franks)

This collection of Breton songs and poems by Théodore Hersart de la Villemarqué, inspired by his interest in the Welsh oral tradition, was produced in 1839. He studied Breton intensively to be able to record the words and music of popular songs, especially in his home area of south Finistère. These are mostly dramatised legends, as performed by story-tellers and bards for entertainment, with French translations given alongside the Breton. He had to publish at his own expense as the French establishment rejected the subject matter. In the 1860s the authenticity of some of the texts was challenged and doubt hung over the reliability of this work for the century that followed, despite acknowledgement of the riches preserved in its pages. In the 1960s, notebooks he had used for research were discovered, and La Villemarqué was largely vindicated. The Barzaz Breiz remains a treasure trove of the popular culture of western Brittany.

Hennebont

Merlevenez

Mané Véchen

Effigy

Jeanne La Flamme

Abbaye Saint-Croix, Quimperlé

Chapelle St-Aubin

Roman bridge, Pont Scorff

Stage 6 ROUTE
Quimperlé to Quimper

We leave the town via the Dourdu valley, and then take a bridge over the busy express way to reach the **Chapelle de la Madeleine**, a former leper-house. Above the west door a tiny figure of the patron Mary Magdalene holds her traditional symbol, a jar of anointing oil. This is not an area of beautiful countryside, being mainly heavily farmed, but the route continues fairly directly, parallel to the express way, before re-crossing it to reach **Le Trévoux**. Here the church, with a pleasant setting beside park and lakes, is dedicated to **Saint Pierre et Saint Paul**. It contains an **allegorical tableau** (1759) of the union of Brittany and France.

The ensuing route to Bannalec by roads through farmland is largely unremarkable, except for the well-kept little **Oratoire Sainte-Anne-des-Bois**, in a small beech grove with seats for contemplation, on what was once the location of a chapel. Even this humble site has a Pardon procession each year in July. In the town of **Bannelec**, the parish church **Église Notre-Dame** in the centre of the town, is usually open for visits.

We now continue across country for nearly 15km, traversing various river valleys and entering an area rich with chapels. Highlights include the very fine and secluded **Chapelle du Moustoir** (16th century) with its exceptionally decorated west door, in a secluded location, and the major site of the **Chapelle de la Trinité** just before Melgven. This sizeable and commanding foundation (also 16th century) has an opulent west porch with a tympanum showing the body of Christ on the knees of God. Inside are ornamental carved beams and rich statuary. The location on the old Roman road from Nantes to Quimper made the chapel an important stage on the early Tro Breiz route.

Continuing the line of this ancient road to the tall Croix de Quinquis, the route then goes on through Kerhuel to **Locmaria-an-Hent**. Here there is a delightfully simple example of the parish close ensemble of religious architecture (see p.147). The **Chapelle Notre-Dame**, with its calvary and delicate ossuary, is also situated on the pilgrim route of the Roman road. An 18th century painted panel inside shows Saint Felicity, a widowed mother of seven sons who defied the Roman authorities in the 2nd century by refusing to deny her Christian faith. She and all her sons were martyred.

After a series of hamlets, the route passes through the Bois de Pleuven and continues by road to **Saint-Évarzec**. (An alternative rural route after the woods via the **Chapelle Sainte Véronique** is an

Chapelle de la Madeleine   *Le Trévoux*

option.) Here the **church is dedicated to Saint Primel**, a Welsh 5th century incomer, who is said to have come to this spot to pray at a primitive oratory. The most precious relic in the treasury here is a fragment of a nail from the cross of the crucifixion. Outside is an ancient tombstone (perhaps 13th century), barely recognisable now, but labelled as a Knights Templar effigy.

The last country section of this stage passes the wood and lake at Le Mur before following a small road all the way to **Ergué-Armel**, a part of Grand Quimper since 1960. The 16th century **Église Saint-Alor** in its well-tended green precinct has the third bishop of Quimper as patron. The *fontaine* was once visited for prayers for rainfall or indications for young women about marrying within the year. They threw in a pin: bad sign if it lay on its side in the water, good if it floated head up!

We now walk into **Quimper** via the grounds of the Château de Lanniron and the ancient quarter of **Locmaria** (see p.134), finally approaching the cathedral in the centre via the banks of the Odet river.

Ossuary, Loc̈maria an Hent

Chapelle du Moustoir

Oratoire Ste-Anne-des-Bois

Saint-Evarzec

St Primel, Saint-Evarzec

Chapelle de la Trinité, Melgven

QUIMPER

The town sits at the confluence (= *kemper* in Breton) of three rivers, the Odet, Steir and Frout, overlooked by the tree-covered Mont Frugy. Little round markers on buildings in the centre show the remarkable heights of flooding since the 1970s. Quimper became the capital of Finistère at the time of the Revolution, when, with the suppression of traditional religion, a Temple of Reason was constructed at the foot of the hill.

The cathedral and medieval centre are a fairly compact unit on the right bank of the river, with a series of **flowery footbridges** over the Odet being the remnant of access for large houses before the riverside road was introduced. The administrative **Prefecture building** beside the river was occupied by the Germans during WWII and burnt down, requiring meticulous restoration.

The oldest settlement was further south on the left bank, where the district of **Locmaria** is today, once the township of the Osismes tribe and later centred on the **Église Notre-Dame de Locmaria**, which is the earliest of all religious foundations in Quimper. A simplicity of architecture, with Romanesque details and the evocative remains of the cloister make this a special place. Close by on banks of the river there is a **medieval-style garden** with healing plants. This was also a thriving industrial quarter and the famous **pottery of Henriot** (started in 1690) still functions today, opposite a museum with some extraordinary examples of this ancient craft.

The historic town and earliest 'cathedral' are said to have been founded in the 5th century by King Gradlon, whose **equestrian statue** now sits between the two lofty towers, which were a 19th century addition. An excellent **museum** is housed in the **Bishop's Palace** next door. Sections of the medieval walls and one defensive **tower** (the **Tour de Nevet**, bounding the secluded **Jardin de la Retraite**) survive. There is a huge variety of domestic architecture from the oldest house (15th century) in rue Treuz to decorative half-timbered dwellings, slate-covered frontages and later stone façades that reduced fire risk. Unusually, the medieval settlement was in the control of the bishop,

River Odet and the Prefecture

Locmaria © D.Wright

Mount Frugy

SANTIG DU

Cathedral

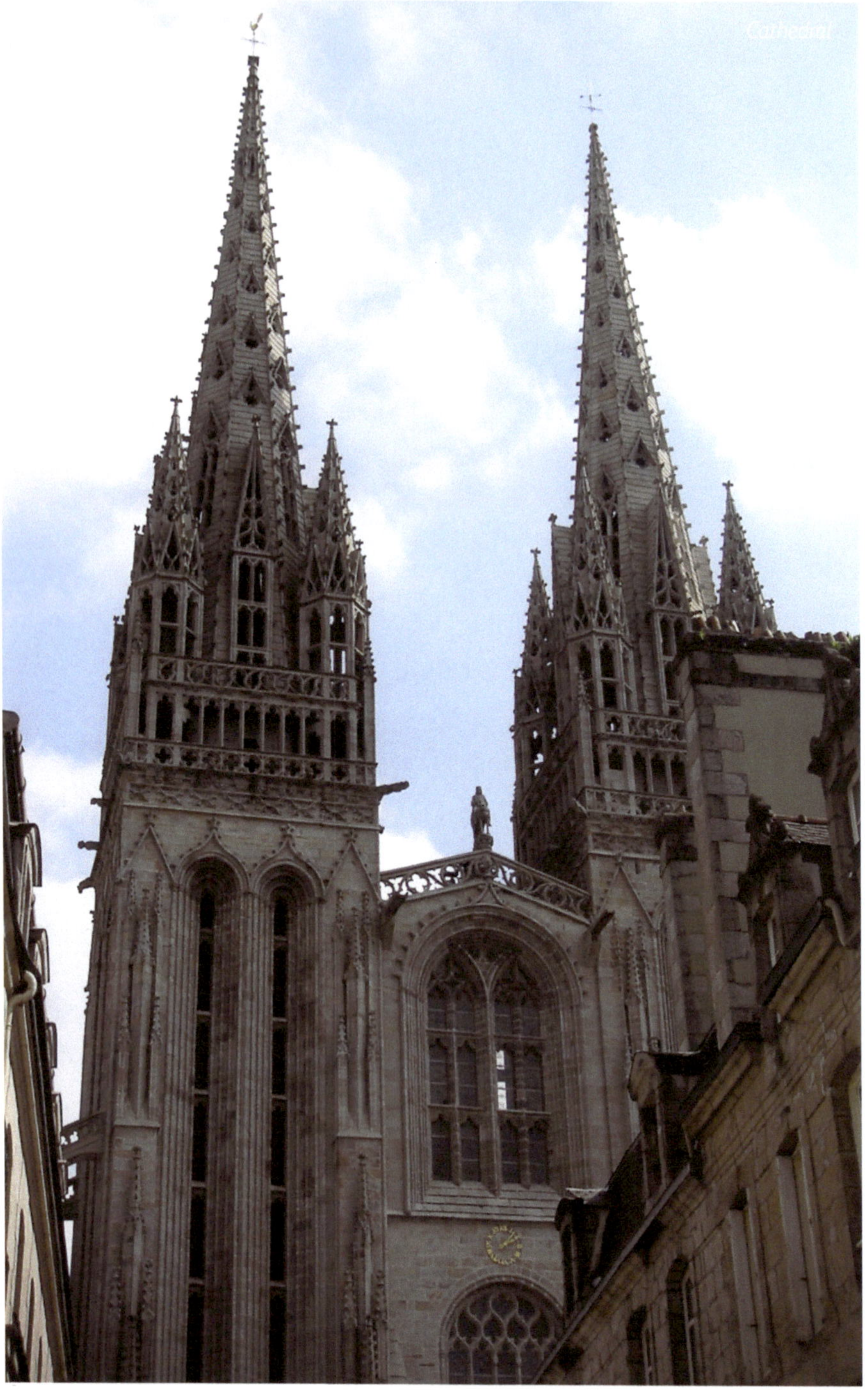

and secular ducal authority only began across the Pont de Médard, where there is an attractive square called **Terre au duc** (Duke's Land).

CATHEDRAL

The glorious Gothic cathedral is dedicated to Saint Corentin, the first bishop of Quimper, after King Gradlon persuaded him to leave his hermit-like existence on Menez Hom (see p.143) and take a more public role in the new city on the banks of the Odet. The current version was founded in 1239, followed by two further main phases of building. On entering by the west door one is immediately aware of the building's unique feature – a **crooked nave**! Explanations for this vary, perhaps it was dictated by conditions for the foundations so close to the river, perhaps because the addition of other buildings prevented a true line when the nave was finally extended after a turbulent 14th century of war and plague.

After the French Revolution, all the wooden statues of saints were carried out of the cathedral into the square and burnt, so many there today have come from elsewhere, like the group showing **Saint Yves** between a rich man and a poor man. **Saint Corentin** has his own chapel, with a stained-glass window showing scenes from his life, including the miraculous fish and an early frying pan! His transition from simple hermit to patron saint of Quimper is portrayed.

A local cult dating back centuries is that of **Santig Du** (Little Black Saint) or Jean Discalceat (John the Barefoot), who was a Franciscan friar (1279-1349). He helped the poor and victims of the plague in Quimper before succumbing himself. It is still traditional to pray to him for help in finding lost things, and to place bread on the table provided below his statue (and reliquary with skull) in thanks when that prayer is answered. Anyone in need today can take the sustenance provided.

Near the entrance is the **tomb of Bishop Adolphe du Parc** (1857-1946), with a frieze of the Seven Founding Saints of Brittany. Some make a rather shorter Tro Breiz by walking around the monument, touching certain points, like his large nose, which are now rather well-worn!

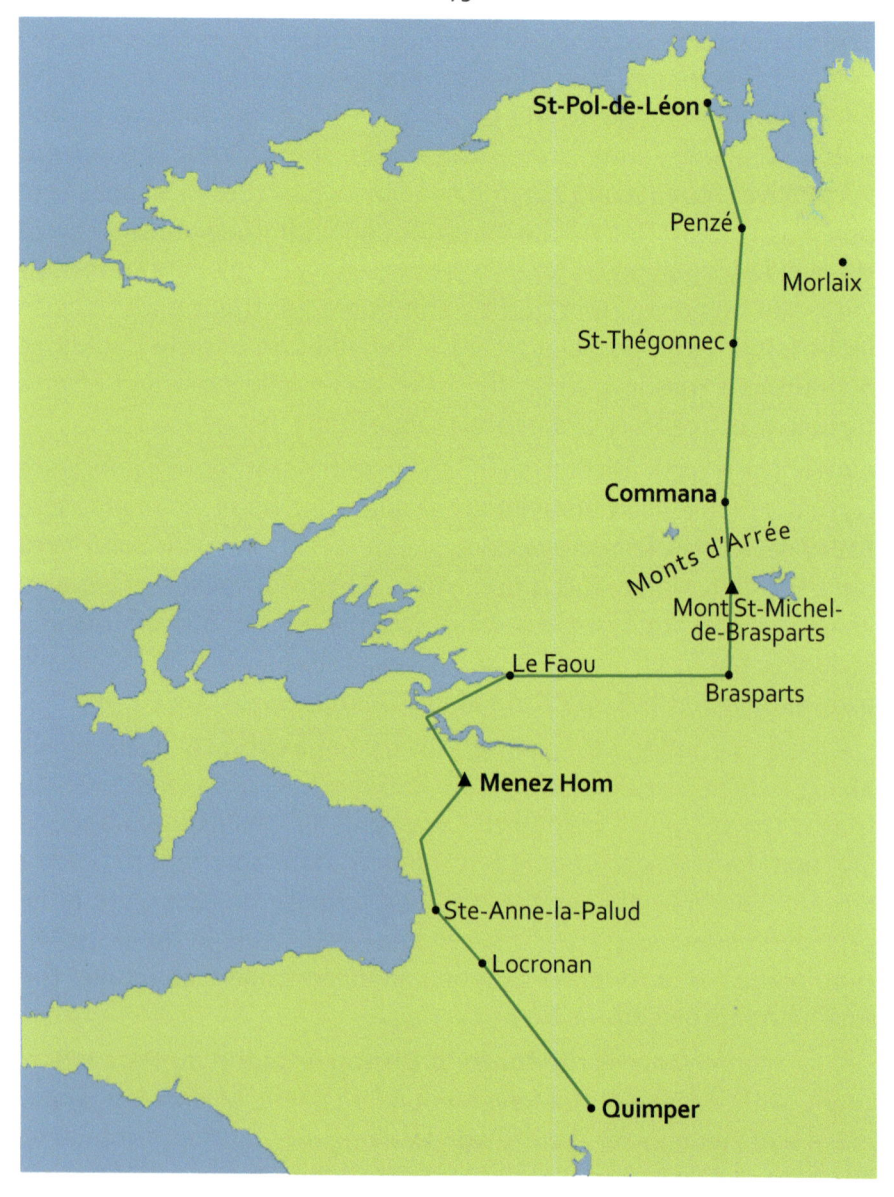

Stage 7
Quimper to Saint-Pol-de-Léon
about 175 kms

Stage 7
Quimper to Saint-Pol-de-Léon

OVERVIEW

The last section of the pilgrimage has the best walking of all. It moves up to the north of Finistère, via the important site of Locronan, and also touches on the Atlantic coast at the famous shrine of Sainte-Anne-la-Palud. There are wonderful views over the ocean and the Bay of Douarnenez from the top of Menez Hom, one of the seven sacred hills of Brittany. Next the route passes through the unique landscape of the Monts d'Arrée with its moors and rocky peaks before entering the region of Léon with some remarkable church architecture. The religious glory of this final stage of the Tro Breiz is undoubtedly the phenomenon of the Parish Closes here.

Monts d'Arrée

Stage 7 ROUTE
Quimper to Menez Hom

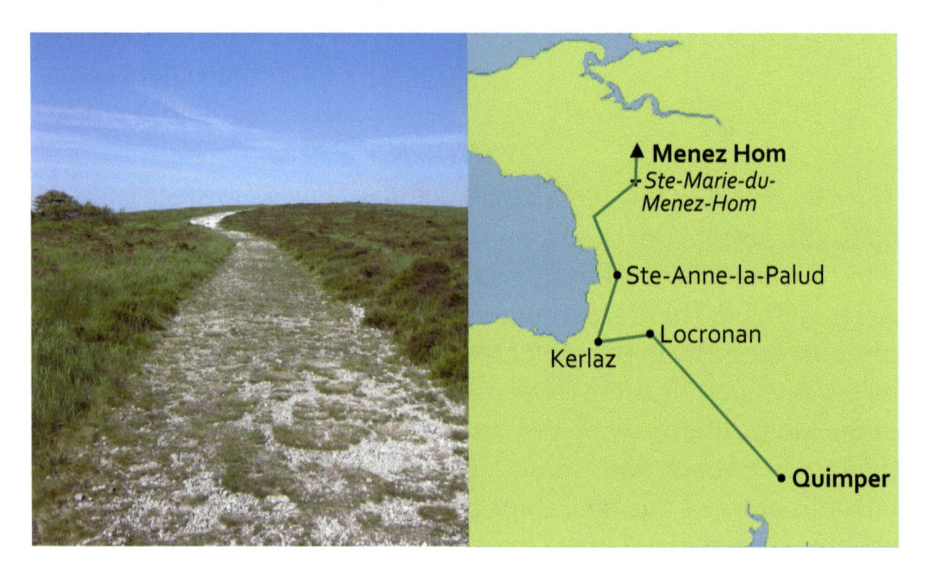

We leave Quimper to the north via the banks of the Steir river, with the path changing sides and then rising as it moves away from the built-up area to wooded hills. Passing the little chapel of St Denis at Seznec, the route continues across country to the Montagne de Locronan. The picturesque Chapelle ar Sonj (chapel of memory, 1977) with its outdoor pulpit, is on the site of an earlier chapel.

Locronan (= sacred place of Ronan) is famous for its 18th century façades and floral displays, often used as a period backdrop in films (such as Roman Polanski's *Tess*). It is a remarkably photogenic place, inevitably now something of a tourist mecca. The main cultural attraction lies in the 15th century **Église Saint Ronan**, with its massive tower and porch over the west door. Inside, a series of medallions on the pulpit shows scenes from Ronan's life. The attached **Chapelle du Pénity** (1530) containing the saint's tomb and effigy, is said to be on the site of his original hermitage.

Saint Ronan came from Ireland in the 6th century and, after a pause north of Brest (the town of Saint-Renan today), he landed his stone boat in the shallow waters of the Bay of Douarnenez. Here he made a controversial start by accusing the locals of being wreckers and had to flee inland. He set up his base in the Bois de Nevet (name from '*nemeton*', a Druid sanctuary), but all did not go smoothly for Ronan as he incurred the jealous wrath of a woman (or witch) called Keben. She accused him of terrible crimes, including murdering her daughter. Ronan was finally forced to flee and eventually died near Hillion in Côtes d'Armor. When the cart bringing his body returned here in Finistère, Keben is said to have broken off the horn of one of the oxen pulling it, hence the name Plas ar horn for the hill above the village. Divine retribution saw Keben swallowed up by a hole in the ground.

The real interest of Locronan lies in the **Tromenie** (from *Tro minihi*, journey around the sacred enclosure), a Pardon held each July, with a **Grand Tromenie** every six years (next in 2025). This covers 12km around the parish with a silent procession carrying banners and statues, passing the twelve stations marked by crosses and dozens of little huts decorated with flowers. It is said that Ronan did this walk every Sunday whilst fasting, stopping to pray at various points, including sacred rocks. The route involves some areas not usually open to the public and it remains open for a week, for those who were unable or unwilling to join the official procession of thousands. In the intervening years, the **Petit Tromenie** is held, covering a 6km circuit. Popular tradition held that doing the Grand Tromenie once or Petit Tromenie three times would ensure a pilgrim's entry to Paradise.

But this is a many-layered site. There are also echoes of earlier pagan beliefs and rituals here, with modern research indicating some relationship with the lunar and solar calendars of the Celts, in the direction of the march and the 12 stations, and celebration of the major Celtic deity Lug. What is sure is that the Tromenie, in superb natural surroundings, can be a profound spiritual experience for any type of pilgrim.

Leaving Locronan past the **Chapelle de Bonne-Nouvelle**, we then continue through the **Bois de Nevet** and via a scenic route to **Kerlaz**. The church here is dedicated to Saint Germain, and has a stained-glass window recalling the visit of fiery preacher Julien Maunoir in 1658. His mission was to bring the faithful back to proper observance of Christian practices, and his tour of the territory had a profound impact on many congregations. Here he is shown addressing the crowd from the *calvaire*.

From here we soon reach the coast and follow the shore all the way to **Sainte Anne la Palud**. This sacred site hosts one of the great Breton Pardons at the end of August each year. The story of Saint

Bay of Douarnenez

Locronan

Tromenie

View from Menez Hom

Anne has many strands and her persona may be an amalgam of different saints. In the Breton legend, she is a native of the region who fled an abusive marriage and ended up in Judaea, where she was to become the mother of the Virgin Mary. According to local tradition, she either came back to live here or revisited the Bay of Douarnenez later. Her grandson Jesus is also said to have paid a visit and caused a spring to flow where the *fontaine* now stands. Anne became known as *Mamm gozh ar Vretoned* (Grandmother of the Bretons), and the cult of this figure from the Apocrypha is an important one in this remote spot behind the dunes. It is a powerful place of pilgrimage. The first shrine was thought to have been built by Saint Guénolé and many versions followed over the next 1500 years. The current chapel contains a famous statue of Saint Anne teaching little Mary to read.

The route continues along the coastal path with wonderful sea views, skirting the shallow Bay of Douarnenez before moving across country to **Sainte-Marie-du-Menez-Hom**. This highly ornate chapel (1570) with its rich statuary, is usually open every day. From here the climb starts to the open hill-top of **Menez Hom**, where the views over land and sea are magnificent. In 1913 a bronze statue of a goddess with a helmet bearing a swan was found by chance near here. It dates to the 1st century CE and has come to be associated with the Celtic goddess Brigid. Today the statue can be seen in the Musée de Bretagne in Rennes.

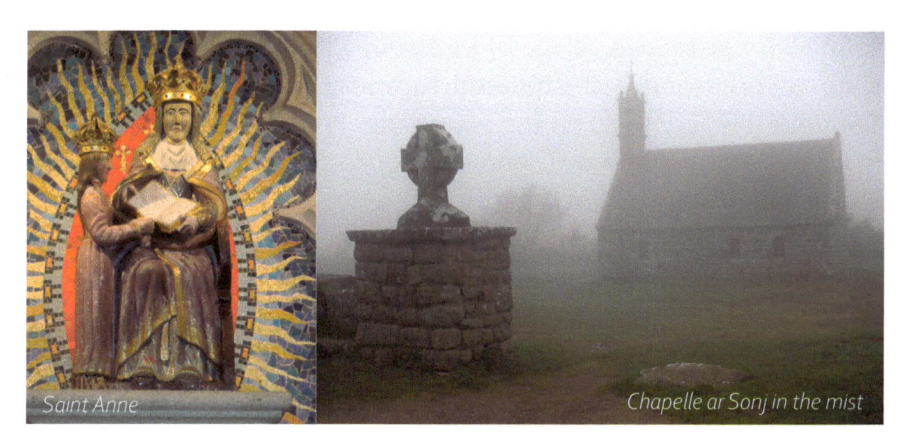

Saint Anne

Chapelle ar Sonj in the mist

Stage 7 ROUTE
Menez Hom to Commana

Mont St-Michel-de-Brasparts

From the height of Menez Hom, the route descends to the Aulne estuary, arriving at the impressive curving **Pont de Térénez** (2011) over the wide river. (Before crossing it is well worth a detour to the ruibs of the **Abbaye de Landévenec**, for the wonderful walk along the estuary and the destination of a medieval site on the banks of the Rade de Brest. There is also an excellent museum of the history of the abbey. A modern Benedictine monastery is on the hillside above the ancient remains.)

Across the bridge, country paths and a section of road walking lead to the very attractive village of **Le Faou**, with its warm stone hues, slate-covered and half-timbered façades, and the **Église Saint-Sauveur** (16th century) on the waterside. From this old port, wood from the nearby Forêt du Cranou was once shipped across the Rade to the naval boatyards of Brest.

We then continue to the remarkable site of **Rumengol**, a few kilometres away. The **Basilica Notre-Dame de Rumengol** (15-18th centuries) was enlarged to accommodate the huge numbers attending one of the most important Pardons in Brittany. A separate Neo-Gothic outdoor chapel was constructed in 1880. In the refulgent church, the window above the high altar depicts the extraordinary foundation legend, with the Virgin Mary sitting on a neolithic dolmen, believed to be a Druid sacrificial stone. Pagan practices on this spot were brought to an end by Saint Guénolé, Saint Corentin and King Gradlon (see p.26), who vowed a chapel on the spot to ensure that Christianity would triumph here. In the foreground of this unusual scene, a Druid with a broken lyre slumps, defeated.

The very rural route goes on through the beautiful **Forêt du Cranou** and then offers an undulating trek to the village of Brasparts, where the handsome **Église Notre-Dame et Saint Tugen** has a faded sculpture of Ankou, the Grim Reaper, on the ossuary building.

From here we ascend via a wooded path and then moorland tracks to the **Monts d'Arrée**, highest hills in Brittany. Here on one of the topmost points, **Mont-Saint-Michel-de-Brasparts** (or Menez Mikel in Breton) we find the landmark **chapel of Saint Michel**, in splendid isolation. This recently renovated building is a symbol of survival in the harsh conditions of this windswept environment. It was used by shepherds in the past for shelter, and there was once a pilgrims' hut to offer refuge to the many brave wayfarers determined to reach this iconic point. The hill was also used by the German occupiers in WWII, as traces of concrete constructions show.

Rough tracks lead us on across the moors and stony ridges, much damaged by terrible fires in 2022, with far-reaching views on all sides. From the height of **Tuchenn Gador**, the small bump of Roc'h Ruz, the very pinnacle of Brittany, can be seen to the right of the communications mast.

Passing across the valley of the Elorn, we descend the northern slopes of the Monts d'Arrée to enter the region of Léon, a fertile contrast to the moors. Here the route passes an exceptional neolithic site, the *allée couverte* **(passage grave)** of **Mougau Bihan**, with its massive stones and interior carvings. Just ahead is the idyllic *fontaine* **and** *lavoir* **of Saint Jean**, before the road leads into the village of **Commana**.

Here is the first of the great Parish Close ensembles (see p.147). This **church** (16-17th centuries) is dedicated to the obscure Saint Derrien, but is famous for the baroque **altarpiece of Saint Anne,** a gilded masterpiece. Outside are two calvaries, an ossuary converted to a chapel (now a shop) and a triumphal entrance gate. The **south porch in Renaissance style** is particularly fine. The spire is austere, designed to stand up to the harsh weather of the Monts d'Arrée.

The Parish Closes

This unique phenomenon of religious architecture can be seen at its best and most prolific in north Finistère. The Tro Breiz route passes Commana, Guimiliau and Saint-Thégonnec in close succession, with each of these three exceptional *enclos paroissiaux* presenting the basic form with very different interpretations.

The parish close is in essence a walled precinct, separating sacred and profane, with a triumphal entrance gate. Inside the enclosure can be found a monumental calvary, often a work of sculptural excellence, and some form of ossuary or bone house. These reminders of death and the potential of resurrection are usually in proximity to the church door, keeping a visual impression of the importance of faith before the congregation. Later sacristies were often added to the body of the church to protect valuables and give church councils privacy for meetings.

Although now rather sombre in appearance, we know that the calvaries and other external decoration of the churches were once painted, bringing a livelier sense to the **enclos**, which was also a focal point of the social life of a village, with weddings, funerals and saints' feast days. The heart of the community was held within the walls. Most of the graveyards have now disappeared to off-site locations, although Commana retains its cemetery beside the church. An elaborately decorated south porch is a feature of the church buildings, with statues of the twelve apostles inside above stone benches where the parish council or *fabrique* used to meet.

The magnificent spires and interiors of the churches reflect the lavish donations prompted by local pride so that each village could have a work of art to match - or preferably outdo - its neighbours. It was indeed a highly competitive issue. The astonishing sumptuousness can be seen in the Altarpiece of Saint Anne in Commana, and the quality of workmanship in the sculpted calvaries of Guimiliau (150 figures) and Saint Thégonnec. The parish closes also brought new styles of art and architecture to western Brittany in line with European trends.

Saint-Thégonnec

The incredible prosperity accrued in Léon by the cloth trade with England (and other countries) accounts for the prevalence of high quality religious structures in this area. All the processes from growing the flax to exporting the finished product from Morlaix took place locally. It was the Breton way to put money into public works, especially churches, rather than ostentatious private houses. Faith was the dominant determinant in this area and a matter of great pride for all the inhabitants of whatever social rank. The parish close was its definitive expression.

Guimiliau

Calvaire, Saint-Thégonnec

Baroque detail

Saint Thégonnec

Noah's Ark, Guimiliau

Stage 7 ROUTE
Commana to Saint-Pol-de-Léon

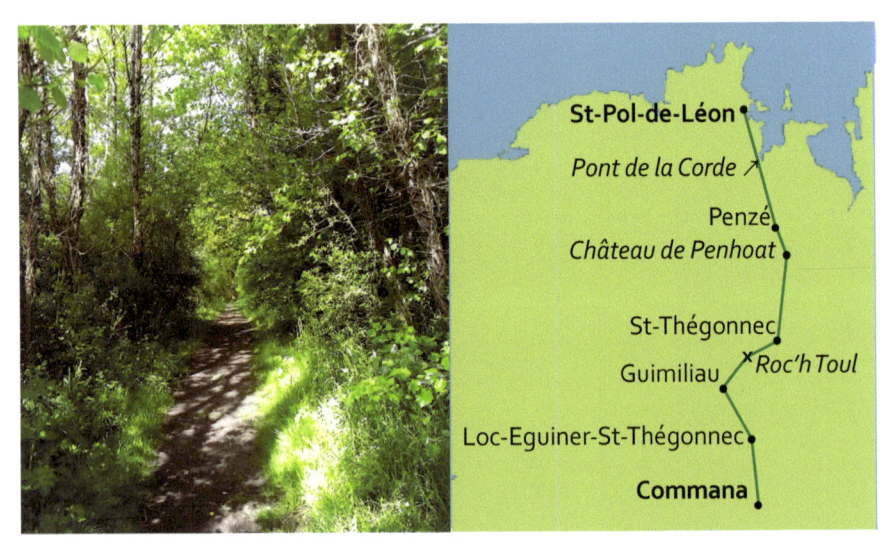

A series of quiet roads leads on towards the village of **Loc-Éguiner** with its prettily situated low **double-naved church and two holy springs**, one dedicated to the eponymous saint Éguiner and the other to Saint Jean. There is also a Christianised Iron Age *stele* in the graveyard.

The route to **Guimiliau** is on a straight track through open farmland before reaching this lovely village with its stunning **Parish Close**. There is also an excellent **interpretation centre** comparing parish closes throughout the area just beyond the precinct. A **Tro Breiz information point**/shop is situated in the main street.

The **Église Saint Miliau** (open every day) contains a painted altarpiece showing scenes from the life and murder of the eponymous saint, who was a local ruler, killed by his brother.

The arch of the entrance porch has some superb carving of scenes from the Old and New Testaments, including an amusing drunken Noah! But the element of greatest renown is the **calvary**, a graphic stone portrayal of scenes from the Passion, but also the local detail of the fate of Katel Gollet, a Breton girl too fond of drink and dancing, pulled down into Hell by demons. A graphic reminder that the calvaries were used by priests as teaching aids. There are 150 people represented in all, plus dozens of strange creatures. It is truly a memorable sight with a delicate finesse of detail.

Some beautiful walking follows with a descent into the Penzé valley past the extremely atmospheric **palaeolithic cave of Roc'h Toul**. A steep climb then takes us to Luzec, past the roadside calvary, and on into the *bourg* of Saint-Thégonnec.

The **parish close of Saint Thégonnec** is the grandest and most visited of them all, with a dramatic architectural statement in the design and execution of the precinct and façade. The triumphal gate, ossuary and bell-tower all give the impression of both immense solidity and upward thrust, with a positive forest of finials. The **calvary** (1610) is superbly expressive in the faces, costumes and posture of the figures. The ossuary has an external statue of Saint Pol and the dragon (see p.38), as we are now once again within the diocesan territory of this founding saint. Inside and out there are representations of Saint Thégonnec himself, shown with a cart. According to legend, a wolf devoured the stag the saint was using to transfer building material for the first church, so Thégonnec ordered the wolf to perform its duties instead. The *enclos* was badly damaged by fire in 1998 and full restoration took seven years.

The route stays beside and around the Penzé after Saint-Thégonnec, with the lonely valley of this sweet-flowing river providing some wonderful walking moments, steeped in nature. On the way are the ruins of the medieval **Château de Penhoat** on its steep hill, a sudden reminder of human presence through history. After the village of Penzé itself and some road walking through farming hamlets, we reach the estuary of the Penzé on its way to join the Morlaix river. A beautiful path past an old *lavoir* leads up to the Pointe de la Corde.

From here, we retrace our steps up the coastal path to Saint-Pol-de-Léon and the original starting point of our journey.

Loc-Eguiner

Château de Penhoat

Pont de la Corde

Return to Saint-Pol-de-Léon

PRACTICAL INFORMATION

Transport

The easiest access to Brittany from the UK is by Brittany Ferries, with sailings from Portsmouth to Saint Malo (the Tro Breiz route passes the ferry port) and Plymouth to Roscoff (a short walk on the coastal path from the ferry port to begin in nearby Saint-Pol-de-Léon).

Website: **brittany-ferries.co.uk** OR **brittany-ferries.fr**

The general journey of the Tro Breiz could be followed in a car between the seven cathedral towns, or, with the odd taxi added, even by train. Public transport in the form of local trains and buses may be helpful in places for walkers (good links by the coast in the tourist season), but there will not be frequent services in rural areas. Taxis must be ordered in advance for collection and drop-off on a day's walk. Accommodation providers may be able to provide this service for a small fee.

Trains (tickets and timetables): **sncf-voyageurs.com**
Regional trains **ter.sncf.com/bretagne**
Overall transport site for Brittany, including buses (remember the French word for a bus is *car*!): **breizhgo.bzh**

Tempted to sample a short trial ?

Stage 4 of the Tro Breiz, the shortest section, could be undertaken in a few days, by crossing to Saint-Malo on Brittany Ferries, walking straight onto the route from the terminal and continuing all the way to Dol-de-Bretagne. From there, return to Saint-Malo by bus or train.

Tourist information

For accommodation, general advice and tourist sites:

Brittany: **tourismebretagne.com**

By department

Finistère: **toutcommenceenfinistere.com**
Côtes d'Armor: **cotesdarmor.com**
Morbihan: **morbihan.com**
Ille-et-Vilaine: **ille-et-vilaine-tourisme.bzh**
(Loire Atlantique: **tourisme-loireatlantique.com**)

Accommodation

Most areas have plenty of *chambres d'hôtes* or B&Bs and campsites. AirB&B is increasingly common. Towns and large villages will have hotels or *auberges*. Note that one night bookings may not always be on offer in high season. Planning and booking ahead really is essential, especially in rural areas, where accommodation may be limited. Religious establishments that welcome pilgrims are mentioned in the Stage sections.

Note that membership of the association Mon Tro Breizh (see p.33-4) gives access to details of accommodation providers on or near the route(s) followed in their guidebooks.

Maps

In addition to the maps in the various guidebooks mentioned, the standard French maps are *Série Bleue* (blue series) from IGN® called *Carte de Randonnée* (with main walking paths marked), offering 1 : 25,000 coverage. They provide valuable back-up and alternatives for the Tro Breiz routes, and can be ordered online at **ign.fr**. The website **geoportail.fr** is a great resource of various maps and aerial views for the whole of Brittany.

Paths

There is an immense variety of paths on the Tro Breiz, as one would expect on so long a pilgrimage. Footpaths (*sentiers*) criss-cross the countryside, reflecting old links between villages, and are often waymarked with yellow slashes, which means a local circuit. More commonly used are tracks (*chemins*), mostly in agricultural use, and plentiful in all areas. (It is perhaps worth noting that footpaths in Brittany very rarely cross fields, and this would often not be acceptable practice – stick to the track alongside the field!)

A major long-distance linear footpath is called GR® (*grand randonnée*, red and white waymarks), and a long-distance circular route exploring a particular area, is GRP® (*grand randonnée de pays*, red and yellow waymarks). **The Tro Breiz is signed in black and white, the newest style of Mon Tro Breizh (see cover) being easily visible. The older versions are different, often faded, and it's important to remember that they may be signing a different route from a previous itinerary.** It helps to carry an IGN® map of the relevant area.

The *Voies Vertes* (Green Ways) are based on former railway lines or canal towpaths, providing often lengthy, unequivocal and easy to walk routes. They form the basis of long-distance bike (*vélo*) routes and cyclists will be in evidence on these trails, which are generally well-signed and maintained.

The Tro Breiz inevitably uses a certain number of roads, whichever way is chosen between the seven cathedrals. Small country lanes pose no problems for walkers, as traffic is sparse and the way often scenic. D roads are main departmental roads which will usually have steady traffic and require care if short sections of passage are necessary. N roads are national dual-carriageways, express routes which the Tro Breiz weaves under and over in a few places.

Please note

It's necessary to understand that chapels in the countryside are usually closed except for certain hours in summer, and even some parish churches in the centre of villages often seem to be locked these days. Enquire at the local town hall (*mairie*) for key-holders, in advance, if seeing inside a particular building is important. Cathedrals and the main parish closes (see p.147) are usually open every day of the year, although renovation work may restrict access at times.

Please think of making a small donation when visiting religious and historical buildings to honour the importance of maintaining these heritage sites.

Other relevant books by the same author:

Brittany: Stone Stories

An Introduction to the Breton Saints

Legends of Brittany

Brittany: a cultural history

Photographs on back cover:

Tréguier cathedral (see p.57)
Temple of Mars, Corseul (see p.75)
Menhir du Champ Dolent (see p.101)
Steps and church at Brélévenez (see p.51)
Bay of St Brieuc (see p.70)
Cross in Bay of Saint-Michel-en-Grève (see p.50)